200 L

cakes & desserts

200 Light
cakes & desserts
hamlyn **all color**

An Hachette UK Company
www.hachette.co.uk

First published in Great Britain in 2015 by Hamlyn
a division of Octopus Publishing Group Ltd,
Endeavour House, 189 Shaftesbury Avenue,
London, WC2H 8JY
www.octopusbooks.co.uk

Distributed in the US by Hachette Book Group
1290 Avenue of the Americas, 4th and 5th Floors
New York, NY 10020

Distributed in Canada by Canadian Manda Group
664 Annette St.,Toronto, Ontario, Canada M6S 2C8

ISBN: 978-0-600-62968-9
Printed and bound in China
10 9 8 7 6 5 4 3 2 1

Standard level kitchen cup and spoon measurements are
used in all recipes.

Ovens should be preheated to the specified temperature;
if using a convection oven, follow the manufacturer's
instructions for adjusting the time and temperature.

Fresh herbs, large eggs, and freshly ground black pepper
should be used unless otherwise stated.

This book contains some dishes made with raw or lightly
cooked eggs. It is prudent for vulnerable people such as
pregnant and nusing mothers, invalids, the elderly, babies,
and young children to avoid uncooked or lightly cooked
dishes made with eggs.

This book includes dishes made with nuts and nut
derivatives. It is advisable for those with known allergic
reactions to nuts and nut derivatives and those who may
be potentially vulnerable to these allergies to avoid dishes
made with nuts and nut oils. It is also prudent to check the
labels of pre-prepared ingredients for the possible inclusion
of nut derivatives.

contents

introduction

introduction

this series

The Hamlyn All Color Light Series is a collection of handy-sized books, each packed with over 200 healthy recipes on a variety of topics and cuisines to suit your needs.

The books are designed to help those people who are trying to lose weight by offering a range of delicious recipes that are low in calories but still high in flavor. The recipes show a calorie count per portion, so you will know exactly what you are eating. These are recipes for real and delicious food, not ultra-slimming meals, so they will help you maintain your new healthier eating plan for life. They must be used as part of a balanced diet, with the cakes and sweet dishes such as the ones in this book eaten only as an occasional treat.

how to use this book

All the recipes in this book are clearly marked with the number of calories (kcal) per serving. The chapters cover different calorie bands: under 500 calories, under 400 calories, etc.

There are variations on each recipe at the bottom of the page—note the calorie count as they do vary and can sometimes be more than the original recipe.

The figures assume that you are using low-fat versions of dairy products, so be sure to use skim milk and low-fat yogurt. Use moderate amounts of oil and butter for cooking and low-fat/low-calorie alternatives when you can.

Don't forget to take note of the number of portions each recipe makes and divide up the quantity of food accordingly, so that you know just how many calories you are consuming.

Be careful about sauces and accompaniments that will add to calorie content.

Above all, enjoy trying out the new flavors and exciting recipes that this book contains. Rather than dwelling on the thought that you are denying yourself your usual unhealthy treats, think of your new regime as a positive step toward a new you. Not only will you lose weight and feel more confident, but your health will benefit, the condition of your hair and nails will improve, and you will take on a healthy glow.

the risks of obesity

Up to half of women and two-thirds of men are overweight or obese in the developed world today. Being overweight can not only make us unhappy with our appearance, but can also lead to serious health problems.

When someone is obese, it means they are overweight to the point that it could start to seriously threaten their health. In fact, obesity ranks as a close second to smoking as a possible cause of cancer. Obese women are more likely to have complications during and after pregnancy, and people who are overweight or obese are also more likely to have coronary heart disease, gallstones, osteoarthritis, high blood pressure, and type 2 diabetes.

how can I tell if I am overweight?

The best way to tell if you are overweight is to work out your body mass index (BMI). If using metric measurements, divide your weight in kilograms (kg) by your height in meters (m) squared. (For example, if you are 1.7 m tall and weigh 70 kg, the calculation would be $70 \div 2.89 = 24.2$.) If using imperial measurements, divide your weight in pounds (lb) by your height in inches (in) squared and multiply by 703. Then compare the figure to the following list (these figures apply to healthy adults only).

Less than 20	underweight
20–25	healthy
25–30	overweight
Over 30	obese

As we all know by now, one of the major causes of obesity is eating too many calories.

what is a calorie?

Our bodies need energy to stay alive, grow, keep warm and be active. We get the energy we need to survive from the food and drinks we consume—more specifically, from the fat, carbohydrate, protein, and alcohol that they contain.

A calorie (cal), as anyone who has ever been on a diet will know, is the unit used to measure

how much energy different foods contain. A calorie can be scientifically defined as the energy required to raise the temperature of 1 gram of water from 14.5°C to 15.5°C. A kilocalorie (kcal) is 1,000 calories and it is, in fact, kilocalories that we usually mean when we talk about the calories in different foods.

Different food types contain different numbers of calories. For example, a gram of carbohydrate (starch or sugar) provides 3.75 kcal, protein provides 4 kcal per gram, fat provides 9 kcal per gram, and alcohol provides 7 kcal per gram.

So, fat is the most concentrated source of energy—weight for weight, it provides just over twice as many calories as protein or carbohydrate—with alcohol not far behind. The energy content of a food or drink depends on how many grams of carbohydrate, fat, protein, and alcohol are present.

how many calories do we need?

The number of calories we need to consume varies from person to person, but your body weight is a clear indication of whether you are eating the right amount. Body weight is simply determined by the number of calories you are eating compared to the number of calories your body is using to maintain itself and needed for physical activity. If you regularly consume more calories than you use up, you will start to gain weight as extra energy is stored in the body as fat.

Based on our relatively inactive modern-day lifestyles, most nutritionists recommend that women should aim to consume around 2,000 calories (kcal) per day, and men around 2,500.

Of course, the amount of energy required depends on your level of activity: the more active you are, the more energy you need to maintain a stable weight.

a healthier lifestyle

To maintain a healthy body weight, we need to expend as much energy as we eat; to lose weight, energy expenditure must exceed calorie intake. So, exercise is a vital tool in the fight to lose weight. Physical activity doesn't just help us control body weight; it also helps to reduce our appetites and is known to have beneficial effects on the heart and blood that help prevent against cardiovascular disease.

Many of us claim we don't enjoy exercise and simply don't have the time to fit it into our hectic schedules. So the easiest way to increase physical activity is by incorporating it into our daily routines, perhaps by walking or cycling instead of driving (particularly for short journeys), taking up more active hobbies, and taking small and simple steps, such as using the stairs instead of the elevator whenever possible.

As a general guide, adults should aim to undertake at least 30 minutes of moderate-intensity exercise, such as a brisk walk, five times a week. This does not have to be all at once: three sessions of 10 minutes are equally beneficial. Children and young people should be encouraged to take at least 60 minutes of moderate-intensity exercise every day.

Some activities will use up more energy than others. The following list shows some examples of the energy a person weighing 132 lb would expend doing the following activities for 30 minutes:

activity	energy
Ironing	69 kcal
Cleaning	75 kcal
Walking	99 kcal
Golf	129 kcal
Fast walking	150 kcal
Cycling	180 kcal
Aerobics	195 kcal
Swimming	195 kcal
Running	300 kcal
Sprinting	405 kcal

make changes for life

The best way to lose weight is to try to adopt healthier eating habits that you can easily maintain all the time, not just when you are trying to slim down. Aim to lose no more than 2 lb per week to ensure you lose only your fat stores. People who go on crash diets

lose lean muscle as well as fat and are much more likely to put the weight back on again soon afterward.

For a woman, the aim is to reduce her daily calorie intake to around 1,500 kcal while she is trying to lose weight, then settle on around 2,000 per day thereafter to maintain her new body weight. Regular exercise will also make a huge difference: the more you can burn, the less you will need to diet.

improve your diet

For most of us, simply adopting a more balanced diet will reduce our calorie intake and lead to weight loss. Follow these simple recommendations:

Eat more starchy foods, such as bread, potatoes, rice, and pasta. Assuming these replace the fattier foods you usually eat, and you don't smother them with oil or butter, this will help reduce the amount of fat and increase the amount of fiber in your diet. As a bonus, try to use wholegrain rice, pasta, and flour, as the energy from these foods is released more slowly in the body, making you feel fuller for longer.

Eat more fruit and vegetables, aiming for at least seven portions of different fruit and vegetables a day (excluding potatoes).

As long as you don't add extra fat to your fruit and vegetables in the form of cream, butter, or oil, these changes will help reduce your fat intake and increase the amount of fiber and vitamins you consume.

Reduce the amount of fat in your diet, so you consume fewer calories. Choosing low-fat versions of dairy products, such as skim milk and low-fat yogurt, doesn't necessarily mean your food will be tasteless. Low-fat versions are available for most dairy products, including milk, cheese, yogurt, and even cream and butter.

Choose lean cuts of meat, such as Canadian bacon instead of regular bacon, and chicken breasts instead of thighs. Trim all visible fat off meat before cooking and avoid frying foods— grill or roast instead. Fish is also naturally low in fat and can make a variety of tempting dishes.

occasional healthy treats

While it is important when trying to lose weight to eat fewer sugary foods, such as cookies, cakes, and chocolate bars, there will be times when a sweet treat is called for: on special occasions and celebrations, for example. If you strive to eat healthily as a matter of course, the occasional dessert or piece of cake becomes a real treat and something to savor. Many of these recipes can be frozen in single portions then defrosted to be enjoyed later (see freezing instructions under "storing cakes" on page 16).

simple steps to reduce your calorie intake

Few of us have an iron will, so when you are trying to cut down make it easier on yourself by following these steps:

- Serve small portions to start with. You may feel satisfied when you have finished, but if you are still hungry you can always go back for more.
- Once you have served up your meal, put away any leftover food before you eat. Don't put heaped serving dishes on the table as you will undoubtedly pick, even if you feel satisfied with what you have already eaten.
- Eat slowly and savor your food; then you are more likely to feel full when you have finished. If you rush a meal, you may still feel hungry afterward.
- Make an effort with your meals. Just because you are cutting down doesn't mean your meals have to be low on taste as well as calories. You will feel more satisfied with a meal you have really enjoyed and will be less likely to look for comfort in a bag of chips or a bar of chocolate.
- Plan your meals in advance to make sure you have all the ingredients you need. Casting around in the pantry when you are hungry is unlikely to result in a healthy, balanced meal.
- Keep healthy and interesting snacks on hand for those moments when you need something to pep you up. You don't need to succumb to a chocolate bar if there are other tempting treats on offer.

Light cakes & desserts

Making your own cakes and desserts is rewarding and relaxing, and though such treats are generally considered off-limits when trying to eat healthily, the recipes in this book include many indulgent favorites that have been given a healthy make-over to keep them under 500, 400, 300, and even 200 calories per portion. These recipes are perfect to turn to when there is something to celebrate or you just feel in need of a treat—sometimes allowing yourself a small indulgence is an

effective way to avoid abandoning a healthy eating regime in disgust. Homemade cakes and desserts surpass any store-bought version, no matter how expensive, and are a highly personal way to spoil family and friends.

baking know-how

preparing your pans

Grease your cake pan by brushing on a little sunflower or vegetable oil, using a pastry brush, or by smearing a small pat of butter thinly over the inside of the pan. Even nonstick pans need a light greasing before use unless fully lined with nonstick parchment paper.

Nonstick parchment paper, as the name suggests, is nonstick and can be used to line pans or baking sheets without the addition of any oil or butter. Wax paper must always be greased after shaping and pressing into a greased pan. It is usually easiest to brush it lightly with a little oil. Nonstick parchment paper is preferable when lining baking sheets for meringues, roasting pans or deep round or square pans, where the base and side are lined.

cooking times

Cooking times are always a guide so do check on your cake's progress during cooking. Rely only on the oven's glass door if possible. Certainly, never open the door until just over halfway through cooking, when the cake will be set and at less risk of sinking. Even then, open it very slightly, just enough to see how

the cake is doing. If it is cooking more quickly at the front or sides, rotate the cake so it cooks evenly.

Cakes should be an even color all over when cooked. Sponge cakes will spring back when gently pressed with fingertips. A toothpick pushed into the middle of larger cakes should come out clean and dry.

pan sizes
Make sure you select the correct size pan for your cake. Pans should be measured across the base, especially if you are using a roasting dish as these normally have slightly sloping sides and a lip on the top edge.

storing cakes
Cakes or cookies are generally best kept in an airtight container and stored in a cool place, but store cakes with cream or cream cheese fillings or frostings in the fridge.

Most cakes freeze well although it's best to freeze those with glacé icing or fresh fruits unfilled or uniced. For very fragile cakes, freeze until firm then wrap in plastic wrap or foil or pack into a plastic container. More robust cakes can be wrapped and then frozen. Large cakes can be sliced before freezing, and the slices interleaved with pieces of nonstick parchment paper, so that just one or two slices can be thawed as required. Use all frozen cakes within 3 months, defrost at room temperature

for 2–4 hours depending on their size. Biscuits and cookies are best refreshed in the oven once defrosted, for 5–10 minutes 350°F.

troubleshooting
If your cake doesn't turn out as expected see if you can identify the problem from the following:

cake cracks heavily on top
- Cake cooked at too high a temperature or on too high an oven shelf.
- Rounded rather than level teaspoons of raising agent were used.
- Too small a pan was used so cake is very deep.

fruit sinks
- Too much fruit for the cake mixture to hold.
- Fruit was damp, or candied cherries, if using, were very sticky with sugar.

cake sinks
- Oven door was opened before cake had set.
- Cake removed from oven before it was cooked right through.
- Too much raising agent so cake rose quickly but then collapsed before mixture was set.

cake does not rise properly
- Air was knocked out—perhaps the flour was stirred into a whisked cake rather than being gently folded in.
- Oven at too low a temperature or was accidentally turned off.

- Leavening agent such as baking powder was forgotten.
- Cake cooked in too large a pan.

cake is dry
- Not enough fat was incorporated.
- Cake was overcooked.
- Not wrapped and stored in a metal or plastic container after baking.

don't forget to …
- Use a pastry brush for greasing cake pans and glazing tops of biscuits.
- Preheat the oven, reducing the temperature by about 25°F if using a fan-assisted oven.
- Center the oven shelf, unless you plan to cook on more than one baking sheet at a time.
- Grease and line the cake pans before you start.
- Use level measuring spoons.
- Use a timer so that you know when to check on the cake's progress.

desserts know-how

whisking eggs and sugar
When making mousses, chilled soufflés, a Jelly roll, or a sponge flan shell, the recipe will call for the eggs and sugar to be whisked until the whisk leaves a trail when lifted above the mixture. This is best done with an handheld electric mixer held over a bowl of eggs and sugar set over a saucepan of gently simmering water. The hot water helps to speed up the whisking process and increase the volume of trapped air in the eggs and sugar.

Three eggs will take 8–10 minutes to whisk until thick. To test when the mixture is ready, lift the beater out of the mixture and try to drizzle a zigzag as the mixture falls from the beater—if this stays on the surface for a few seconds, the mixture is ready.

whipping cream
Many people tend to overwhip heavy or whipping cream. The secret is to whip the cream until it just begins to form soft swirls, as it will thicken slightly as it stands. Overwhipping makes the cream take on a grainy, almost buttery texture and spoils the finish of the dessert.

folding in
Once a whisked mixture is ready, you will need to fold in pureed fruit, whipped cream, or melted chocolate for a chilled soufflé or mousse, or sifted flour for a whisked sponge. Use a large-bowled spoon (a serving spoon is ideal) and gently cut and turn the spoon through the mixture in a figure-of-eight movement. Try to be as gentle as you can so that you don't knock out all the air you have just worked so hard to incorporate.

sugars
Superfine sugar is preferred for some recipes. If you cannot find this, you can easily make it at home by blending granulated sugar in a food processor for 1 minute.

recipes
under 200
calories

french macaroons

Calories per serving **46**
Makes **24**
Preparation time **20 minutes**,
  plus standing
Cooking time **10 minutes**

butter, for greasing
½ cup **confectioners' sugar**
½ cup **ground almonds**
2 **egg whites**
½ cup **superfine sugar**
pink and **green food coloring**

Grease 2 baking sheets and line with nonstick parchment paper.

Put the confectioners' sugar in a food processor with the ground almonds and blend to a very fine consistency.

Put the egg whites in a thoroughly clean bowl and whisk until stiffly peaking. Gradually whisk in the superfine sugar, a tablespoonful at a time and whisking well after each addition, until thick and very glossy. Divide the mixture equally between 2 bowls and add a few drops of food coloring to each bowl. Divide the almond mixture equally between the 2 bowls and use a metal spoon to stir the mixtures gently to combine.

Place 1 color in a pastry bag fitted with a ½ inch plain tip and pipe 1¼ inch circles onto 1 baking sheet. Tap the baking sheet firmly to smooth the surfaces of the macaroons. Wash and dry the bag and piping tip and pipe 12 circles in the second color onto the other baking sheet. Let stand for 30 minutes.

Bake in a preheated oven, at 325°F, for about 15 minutes or until the surfaces feel crisp. Let cool before carefully peeling away the paper.

pistachio biscotti

Calories per serving **53**

Makes about **24**

Preparation time **15 minutes**,
  plus cooling

Cooking time **30 minutes**

2 tablespoons **slightly salted
  butter**, softened

¼ cup **superfine sugar**

finely grated zest of 1 **lemon**

1 cup **all-purpose flour**

1½ teaspoons **baking powder**

1 **egg yolk**

1 tablespoon **egg white**

½ cup **shelled pistachio
  nuts**, skinned and roughly
  chopped

Beat together the butter, sugar, and lemon zest
in a bowl until pale and fluffy. Sift in the flour and
baking powder, then add the egg yolk, egg white, and
pistachios and mix to a soft dough.

Divide the dough into 2 pieces and shape each into
a sausage about 6 inches long. Place the pieces, well
spaced apart, on a greased baking sheet and flatten
each to a depth of ½ inch.

Bake in a preheated oven, at 325°F, for 20 minutes,
until risen and turning pale golden. Remove from the
oven and let cool for 10 minutes, leaving the oven on.
Using a serrated knife, cut the biscotti across into
½ inch thick slices. Return to the baking sheet, cut
sides face up, and bake for an additional 10 minutes
to crisp up. Transfer to a wire rack to cool.

For walnut oat cookies, mix together ⅓ cup sifted
all-purpose flour, ½ cup rolled oats, ¼ cup chopped
walnuts, ¼ teaspoon baking powder, and ¼ teaspoon
baking soda in a bowl. Put 3½ tablespoons slightly
salted butter, ¼ cup unrefined superfine sugar, and
1 tablespoon light corn syrup in a small saucepan.
Heat gently until the butter has melted. Add to the
oat mixture and stir well to mix. Roll teaspoonfuls of
the mixture into small balls and space well apart on
a greased baking sheet. Bake as above for about
15 minutes, until pale golden. Transfer to a wire rack
to cool. **Calories per serving 53**

triple chocolate pretzels

Calories per serving **54**
Makes **40**
Preparation time **30 minutes**,
  plus rising and setting
Cooking time **6–8 minutes**

1²/₃ cups **white bread flour**
1 teaspoon **active dry yeast**
2 teaspoons **superfine sugar**
large pinch of **salt**
1 tablespoon melted **butter**
  or **sunflower oil**
½ cup warm **water**
3 oz each **semisweet**, **white**,
  and **milk chocolate**, broken
  into pieces

Glaze
2 tablespoons **water**
½ teaspoon **salt**

Mix the flour, yeast, sugar, and salt in a mixing bowl. Add the melted butter or oil and gradually mix in the warm water until you have a smooth dough. Knead the dough for 5 minutes on a lightly floured surface, until smooth and elastic.

Cut the dough into quarters, then cut each quarter into 10 smaller pieces. Shape each piece into a thin rope about 8 inches long. Bend the rope so that it forms a wide arc, then bring one of the ends round in a loop and secure about halfway along the rope. Do the same with the other end, looping it across the first secured end.

Transfer the pretzels to 2 large greased baking sheets. Cover loosely with lightly oiled plastic wrap and leave in a warm place for 30 minutes until well risen.

Make the glaze. Mix the water and salt in a bowl until the salt has dissolved, then brush this over the pretzels. Bake in a preheated oven, at 400°F, for 6–8 minutes, until golden brown. Transfer to a wire rack to cool.

Melt the different chocolates in 3 separate heatproof bowls set over saucepans of gently simmering water. Drizzle random lines of semisweet chocolate over the pretzels, using a spoon. Let harden, then repeat with the white and then the milk chocolate.

For classic pretzels, brush plain pretzels as soon as they come out of the oven with a glaze made by heating 2 teaspoons salt, ½ teaspoon superfine sugar, and 2 tablespoons water in a saucepan until dissolved. **Calories per serving 22**

24

blueberry friands

Calories per serving **65**
Makes **16**
Preparation time **10 minutes**
Cooking time **15 minutes**

3½ tablespoons **lightly salted butter**
2 **egg whites**
¼ cup **all-purpose flour**
⅔ cup **confectioners' sugar**, plus extra for dusting
⅓ cup **ground almonds**
½ teaspoon **almond extract**
½ cup **blueberries**

Place 16 mini silicone muffin liners on a baking sheet.

Melt the butter and let cool. Whisk the egg whites in a thoroughly clean bowl until frothy but not turning white and peaking.

Sift the flour and confectioners' sugar into the bowl, then add the ground almonds. Stir the almond extract into the melted butter and add to the bowl. Using a large metal spoon, stir the ingredients gently together until combined. Divide among the cases so each is about three-quarters full and place several blueberries on top of each.

Bake in a preheated oven, at 400°F, for 12–15 minutes, until risen and just firm to the touch. Leave in the liners for 5 minutes, then transfer to a wire rack to cool. Serve warm or cold, dusted with confectioners' sugar.

For hazelnut & apricot friands, lightly toast ⅓ cup hazelnuts and zest in a food processor. Chop ⅓ cup plump dried apricots into very small pieces. Prepare the cakes as above using the hazelnuts instead of the almonds, vanilla extract instead of the almond extract, and placing a little pile of chopped apricots in the centers instead of the blueberries. **Calories per serving 70**

seeded oatcakes

Calories per serving **65**
Makes **20**
Preparation time **15 minutes**
Cooking time **25 minutes**

¾ cup **steel-cut oats**

⅔ cup **all-purpose flour**

4 tablespoons **mixed seeds**, such as **poppy seeds**, **flaxseeds**, and **sesame seeds**

½ teaspoon **celery salt** or **sea salt**

½ teaspoon **freshly ground black pepper**

3½ tablespoons **unsalted butter**, chilled and diced

5 tablespoons **cold water**

Put the oats, flour, seeds, salt, and pepper in a bowl or food processor. Add the butter and blend with the fingertips or process until the mixture resembles bread crumbs. Add the measured water and mix or blend to a firm dough, adding a little more water if the dough feels dry.

Roll out the dough on a lightly floured surface to ⅛ inch thick. Cut out 20 circles using a 2½ inch plain or fluted cookie cutter, rerolling the trimmings to make more. Place slightly apart on a large greased baking sheet.

Bake in a preheated oven, at 350°F, for about 25 minutes, until firm. Transfer to a wire rack to cool. Serve with cheese.

For crushed spice crackers, crush ½ teaspoon cumin seeds, ½ teaspoon coriander seeds, and ¼ teaspoon dried red pepper flakes using a mortar and pestle or a small bowl and the end of a rolling pin. Finely chop 2 tablespoons ready-to-eat dried apricots. Make as above, omitting the seeds and celery salt and adding the crushed spices and apricots. Serve with soft cheeses. **Calories per serving 59**

lemon & cardamom madeleines

Calories per serving **80**

Makes **about 30**

Preparation time **20 minutes,**
plus setting

Cooking time **30 minutes**

1 stick **lightly salted butter,**
melted, plus extra for
greasing

1 cup **all-purpose flour**, plus
extra for dusting

2 teaspoons **cardamom pods**

3 **eggs**

⅔ cup **superfine sugar**

finely grated zest of 1 **lemon**

1½ teaspoons **baking powder**

Glaze

2 tablespoons **lemon juice**

¾ cup **confectioners' sugar,**
sifted, plus extra for dusting

Grease a madeleine pan with melted butter and dust with flour. Tap out the excess flour.

Crush the cardamom pods using a mortar and pestle to release the seeds. Remove the shells and crush the seeds a little more.

Put the eggs, superfine sugar, lemon zest, and crushed cardamom seeds in a heatproof bowl and rest the bowl over a saucepan of gently simmering water. Whisk with a handheld electric mixer until the mixture is thick and pale and leaves a trail when lifted.

Sift the flour and baking powder into the bowl and gently fold in using a large metal spoon. Drizzle the melted butter around the edges of the batter and fold the ingredients together to combine. Spoon the batter into the madeleine molds until about two-thirds full. (Keep the remaining mixture for a second batch.)

Bake in a preheated oven, at 425°F, for about 10 minutes, until risen and golden. Leave in the pan for 5 minutes, then transfer to a wire rack.

Place the lemon juice in a bowl and beat in the confectioners' sugar. Brush the glaze over the madeleines and let set. Serve lightly dusted with confectioners' sugar.

For espresso madeleines with coffee glaze, mix 1 teaspoon instant espresso coffee powder with 2 teaspoons hot water. Make the madeleines, adding the coffee mixture once the beater leaves a trail. Bake as above. Mix ½ teaspoon espresso coffee powder with 2 teaspoons hot water. Beat with ½ cup sifted confectioners' sugar until smooth and brush over the madeleines. **Calories per serving 76**

raspberry ripple meringues

Calories per serving **81**

Makes about **12**

Preparation time **15 minutes**

Cooking time **1¼ hours**

⅓ cup **fresh raspberries**, plus extra to serve (optional)

2 tablespoons **raspberry jelly**

4 **egg whites**

1 cup **superfine sugar**

Put the raspberries in a bowl and mash with a fork until broken up and turning juicy. Add the jelly and mash together to make a puree. Tip into a sieve resting over a small bowl and press the puree with the back of a spoon to extract as much juice as possible.

Whisk the egg whites in a large clean bowl with a handheld electric mixer until peaking. Whisk in a tablespoonful of the sugar and continue to whisk for about 15 seconds. Gradually add the remaining sugar, a spoonful at a time, until thick and glossy.

Drizzle over the raspberry puree and lightly stir in using a spatula or large metal spoon, scooping up the meringue from the base of the bowl so that the mixture is streaked with the puree. Take care not to overmix.

Drop large spoonfuls of the mixture, each about the size of a small orange, onto a large baking sheet lined with parchment paper, then swirl with the back of a teaspoon. Bake in a preheated oven, at 250°F, for about 1¼ hours or until the meringues are crisp and come away easily from the paper. Leave to cool on the paper. Serve with extra raspberries, if desired.

For gingerbread meringues, put 5 tablespoons molasses in a small bowl, stir in 2 teaspoons ground ginger, 1 teaspoon ground pumpkin pie spice, and 1 teaspoon boiling water and mix well. Make the meringue mixture as above, replacing ¼ cup of the superfine sugar with ¼ cup dark brown sugar, then ripple with the molasses syrup instead of the raspberry puree. Bake as above. **Calories per serving 93**

fresh melon sorbet

Calories per serving **86**
Serves **4**
Preparation time **15 minutes**,
  plus freezing

1 **cantaloupe melon**,
  weighing 2 lb
½ cup **confectioners' sugar**
juice of 1 **lime** or **small lemon**
1 **egg white**

Cut the melon in half and scoop out and discard the seeds. Scoop out the melon flesh with a spoon and discard the shells.

Place the flesh in a food processor or blender with the confectioners' sugar and lime or lemon juice and process to a puree. (Alternatively, rub through a sieve.) Pour into a freezer container, cover, and freeze for 2–3 hours.

If using an ice-cream machine, puree, then pour into the machine, churn and freeze until half-frozen.

Beat the melon mixture to break up the ice crystals. Then whisk the egg white until stiff and whisk it into the half-frozen melon mixture. Return to the freezer until firm. Alternatively, add whisked egg white to the ice-cream machine and churn until very thick.

Transfer the sorbet to the fridge 20 minutes before serving to soften slightly or scoop straight from the ice-cream machine. Scoop the sorbet into glass dishes to serve. To make differently colored sorbet, make up three batches of sorbet using a cantaloupe melon in one and honeydew and watermelon in the others.

For gingered melon sorbet, peel and finely grate a 1 inch piece of ginger root, then stir into the melon puree. Scoop into small glasses and drizzle each glass with 1 tablespoon ginger wine. **Calories per serving 92**

fruited griddle cakes

Calories per serving **86**
Makes **30**
Preparation time **25 minutes**
Cooking time **18 minutes**

2 cups **all-purpose flour**
2 teaspoons **baking powder**
1 stick **butter**, diced
½ cup **superfine sugar**, plus
   extra for sprinkling
⅓ cup **currants**
⅓ cup **golden raisins**
1 teaspoon **ground pumpkin
   pie spice**
grated zest of ½ **lemon**
1 **egg**, beaten
1 tablespoon **milk**, if needed
oil, for greasing

Put the flour and baking powder in a mixing bowl or a food processor. Add the butter and blend with your fingertips or process until the mixture resembles fine bread crumbs. Stir in the sugar, dried fruit, spice, and lemon zest.

Add the egg, then gradually mix in milk, if needed, to make a smooth dough. Knead lightly, then roll out on a lightly floured surface until ¼ inch thick. Stamp out 2 inch circles using a fluted round cookie cutter. Reknead the trimmings and continue rolling and stamping out until all the dough has been used.

Pour a little oil onto a piece of folded paper towel and use to grease a griddle or heavy nonstick skillet. Heat the skillet, then add the cakes in batches, regreasing the griddle or skillet as needed, and fry over medium to low heat for about 3 minutes each side, until golden brown and cooked through. Serve warm, sprinkled with a little extra sugar or spread with butter, if desired. Store in an airtight container for up to 2 days.

For orange & cinnamon griddle cakes, use the grated zest of ½ orange instead of the lemon, and 1 teaspoon ground cinnamon in place of the pumpkin pie spice. Continue the recipe as above. **Calories per serving 86**

honey, grape & cinnamon tartlets

Calories per serving **96**
Makes **16**
Preparation time **25 minutes,**
  plus cooling
Cooking time **10 minutes**

½ cup **seedless red grapes,**
  peeled and halved
½ cup **seedless white**
  grapes, peeled and halved
3 tablespoons **dessert wine**
  or **grape juice**
2 tablespoons **unsalted**
  butter, melted
½ teaspoon **ground**
  cinnamon
3 sheets of **phyllo pastry**
flour, for dusting
scant ½ cup **heavy cream**
scant ½ cup **Greek yogurt**
2 tablespoons **honey**, plus
  extra to drizzle

Place 16 mini silicone muffin liners on a baking sheet.

Put the grapes in a bowl with the wine or grape juice. Mix the melted butter with the cinnamon.

Unfold the pastry sheets on a lightly floured surface, then put one in front of you (covering the others with plastic wrap). Cut into 2¾ inch squares. Brush the squares lightly with the spiced butter. Cut out more squares from the other 2 sheets and position over the first, adjusting the positions so the points are evenly staggered. Press into the liners and brush with a little more butter.

Bake in a preheated oven, at 375°F, for 10 minutes, until golden. Transfer to a wire rack.

Beat the cream with the yogurt and honey until just holding its shape. Drain the grapes over the cream so you can beat the juice into the cream. Spoon the cream mixture into the pastry shells and pile the grapes on top. Serve drizzled with extra honey.

For blueberry & cream cheese tartlets, make the phyllo shells as above, omitting the cinnamon from the butter. Beat 1 cup cream cheese in a bowl with 1 teaspoon vanilla bean paste and 2 tablespoons sifted confectioners' sugar until smooth. Spoon into the shells and top with blueberry preserves. Serve lightly dusted with confectioners' sugar. **Calories per serving 102**

easy almond macaroons

Calories per serving **98**
Makes about **15**
Preparation time **10 minutes**
Cooking time **15 minutes**

2 **egg whites**
½ cup **unrefined superfine
    sugar**
1 cup **ground almonds**
blanched almonds, to
    decorate

Whisk the egg whites in a clean bowl with a handheld electric mixer until peaking. Gradually whisk in the sugar, a spoonful at a time, until thick and glossy. Add the ground almonds and stir in until combined.

Drop dessertspoonfuls of the mixture, slightly apart, on a large baking sheet lined with parchment paper. Press an almond on top of each.

Bake in a preheated oven, at 350°F, for about 15 minutes, until the cookies are pale golden and just crisp. Leave on the paper for 5 minutes, then transfer to a wire rack to cool.

For scribbled chocolate macaroons, make the macaroons as above, replacing 3 tablespoons of the ground almonds with 3 tablespoons unsweetened cocoa powder and omitting the whole almonds. Melt 2 oz semisweet dark or milk chocolate, then drizzle over the cooled cookies with a teaspoon. **Calories per serving 103**

balsamic strawberries & mango

Calories per serving **100**

Serves **4**

Preparation time **5 minutes**, plus overnight chilling and standing

3 cups **strawberries**, thickly sliced

1 large **mango**, peeled, pitted, and sliced

1–2 tablespoons **sugar**, to taste

3 tablespoons **balsamic vinegar**

2 tablespoons chopped **fresh mint**, to decorate

Mix together the strawberries and mango in a large, shallow bowl, sprinkle with the sugar, according to taste, and pour over the balsamic vinegar. Cover with plastic wrap and chill overnight.

Remove the fruit from the refrigerator and let stand for at least 1 hour before serving.

Spoon the fruit into serving bowls, drizzle over the syrup and serve, sprinkled with the mint.

For peppery strawberries & blueberries, mix the strawberries with 1 cup blueberries and make as above. Sprinkle with a few grinds of black pepper and the chopped mint before serving. **Calories per serving 76**

marshmallow crackle squares

Calories per serving **102**

Cuts into **14**

Preparation time **10 minutes**, plus setting

Cooking time **5 minutes**

2 cups **marshmallows**, halved

3 tablespoons **unsalted butter**, diced

3¾ cups **crisped rice cereal**

pink sugar sprinkles, to decorate

Reserve 2 oz of the marshmallows. Put 2 tablespoons of the butter and the remaining marshmallows into a saucepan and heat very gently until melted. Remove from the heat and stir in the cereal until evenly coated.

Spoon the mixture into a 7 inch square shallow baking pan, greased and lined with parchment paper, and pack down firmly with the back of a lightly oiled spoon.

Place the remaining butter and reserved marshmallows in a small saucepan and heat gently until melted. Drizzle into the pan in lines, then scatter the sprinkles over the top. Leave in a cool place for 2 hours or until firm. Turn out of the pan onto a board, peel off the lining paper, and cut into small squares.

For chocolate crackle cakes, melt 3½ oz milk chocolate, broken into pieces, and 1 tablespoon light corn syrup in a heatproof bowl set over a saucepan of gently simmering water (don't let the base of the bowl touch the water). Put 4 cups cornflakes in a plastic bag and crush lightly using a rolling pin. Tip into the chocolate mixture and stir well until thoroughly combined. Pack into 14–16 small paper cupcake liners and top with chocolate sprinkles. Leave to set for at least 1 hour before serving. **Calories per serving 79**

figs with yogurt & honey

Calories per serving **105**
Serves **4**
Preparation time **5 minutes**
Cooking time **10 minutes**

8 ripe **figs**
4 tablespoons **plain yogurt**
2 tablespoons **honey**

Slice the figs in half and place on a hot ridged grill pan, skin-side down. Sear for 10 minutes until the skins begin to blacken, then remove.

Arrange the figs on 4 plates and serve with a spoonful of yogurt and some honey spooned over the top.

For brioche French toasts with figs, yogurt & honey, brush 4 slices brioche with a mixture of 3½ tablespoons melted butter and 3½ tablespoons light cream and toast under a broiler. Top with figs, as above. **Calories per serving 347**

poached peaches & raspberries

Calories per serving **107**
Serves **6**
Preparation time **15 minutes**
Cooking time **25 minutes**

1 cup **water**
²/₃ cup **marsala** or **sweet sherry**
¹/₃ cup **sugar**
1 **vanilla bean**
6 **peaches**, halved and pitted
1¼ cups **fresh raspberries**

Pour the measured water and marsala or sherry into a saucepan, then add the sugar. Slit the vanilla bean lengthwise and scrape out the black seeds from inside the pod. Add these to the water with the pod, then gently heat the mixture until the sugar has dissolved.

Place the peach halves in an ovenproof dish so that they sit together snugly. Pour over the hot syrup, then cover and cook in a preheated oven, at 350°F, for 20 minutes.

Sprinkle over the raspberries. Serve the fruit either warm or cold. Spoon into serving bowls and decorate with the vanilla bean cut into thin strips.

For poached prunes with vanilla, make the sugar syrup as above, then add 1½ cups dried pitted prunes instead of the peaches. Cover and simmer as above, then serve warm with spoonfuls of reduced-fat sour cream and 4 crumbled amaretti cookies, if desired. Calories per serving 156 (not including sour cream and amaretti)

scrabble cookies

Calories per serving **108**
Makes **30**
Preparation time **35 minutes**
Cooking time **5 minutes**, plus
  chilling and cooling

5 tablespoons **unsalted
  butter**, softened, plus extra
  for greasing
1/3 cup **superfine sugar**
1 egg
1/2 teaspoon **vanilla extract**
2 cups **all-purpose flour**,
  sifted, plus extra for dusting

To decorate
12 oz **ready-to-use fondant**
confectioners' sugar, for
  dusting
2–3 tablespoons **apricot
  preserves**, sieved
1 small tube of **colored
  decorator icing**

Grease 2 baking sheets and line with nonstick
parchment paper. Beat together the butter and sugar
until pale and fluffy. Gradually beat in the egg and
vanilla extract, adding a little flour to prevent the mixture
curdling. Add the flour and fold in to make a stiff dough.
Wrap in plastic wrap and refrigerate for 20 minutes.

Roll out the dough on a lightly floured surface to
1/8 inch thick. Cut out about 30 circles, using a
1 1/2–2 inch diameter cookie cutter, rerolling the
trimmings as necessary. Place on the baking sheets.

Bake in a preheated oven, at 350°F, for 5 minutes or
until a pale golden color. Transfer to a wire rack and let
cool. Roll out the fondant on a sugar-dusted surface
until 1/8 inch thick. Using the same cutter as before,
dusted this time with a little confectioners' sugar, cut out
the same number of circles. Using a clean paintbrush,
paint a little of the sieved preserves on each cookie to
ensure that the fondant will stick, then place the fondant
shapes on the cookies and press down lightly. Using the
colored decorator icing, write a letter on each cookie to
spell out the name or message.

For homemade ready-to-use fondant, put 1 tablespoon
egg white in a bowl with 1 tablespoon glucose syrup
and 1 cup sifted confectioners' sugar and beat to a
smooth paste. Gradually work in an additional 1 1/2 cups
confectioners' sugar, stirring well until the mixture is
very firm. Turn out onto the work surface and knead
to a smooth paste, which should be firm and rollable,
not sticky. Work in a little more confectioners' sugar if
necessary. Wrap tightly in several thicknesses of plastic
wrap and store until ready. **Calories per serving 33**

banana & raisin drop scones

Calories per serving **110**
Makes **10**
Preparation time **10 minutes**
Cooking time **8 minutes**

1 cup **all-purpose flour**
2 tablespoons **superfine
    sugar**
1½ teaspoons **baking powder**
1 small ripe **banana**, about
    4 oz with skin on, peeled
    and roughly mashed
1 **egg**, beaten
⅔ cup **milk**
⅓ cup **golden raisins**
oil, for greasing
butter, **honey**, **light corn** or
    maple syrup, to serve

Put the flour, sugar, and baking powder in a mixing
bowl. Add the mashed banana with the egg. Gradually
beat in the milk with a fork until the mixture resembles
a smooth thick batter. Stir in the golden raisins.

Pour a little oil onto a piece of folded paper towel
and use to grease a griddle or heavy nonstick skillet.
Heat the pan, then drop heaping dessertspoonfuls
of the mixture, well spaced apart, onto the pan. Cook
for 2 minutes, until bubbles appear on the top and
the undersides are golden. Turn over and cook for
1–2 minutes more until the second side is done.

Serve warm, topped with 1 teaspoon butter, honey,
light corn or maple syrup per scone. These are best
eaten on the day they are made.

For summer berry drop scones, make the above
recipe in the same way but stir in 1 cup mixed fresh
blueberries and raspberries instead of the golden
raisins. **Calories per serving 101**

banana & brown sugar ripples

Calories per serving **112**
Serves **4**
Preparation time **5 minutes**,
  plus standing

2 ripe **bananas**
juice of ½ **lemon**
1½ tablespoons finely
  chopped crystallized or
  candied **ginger**, plus extra
  to decorate
⅔ cup **low-fat plain yogurt**
8 teaspoons firmly packed
  dark brown sugar

Toss the bananas in a little lemon juice and mash on a plate with a fork. Add the ginger and yogurt and mix together. Spoon one-third of the mixture into the bases of 4 small dessert glasses.

Sprinkle 1 teaspoon of the sugar over each dessert. Spoon half of the remaining banana mixture on top, then repeat with a second layer of sugar. Complete the layers with the remaining banana mixture and decorate with a little extra ginger, cut into slightly larger pieces.

Let the desserts stand for 10–15 minutes for the sugar to dissolve and form a syrupy layer between the layers of banana yogurt. Serve with dainty cookies, if desired.

For banana, apricot & cardamom ripples, cook ⅔ cup ready-to-eat dried apricots with ⅔ cup water and 2 roughly crushed cardamom pods, adding the pods and their black seeds, in a covered saucepan for 10 minutes until tender. Remove and discard the cardamom pods, then puree the mixture with 3 tablespoons fresh orange juice. Cool, then layer with banana and the yogurt mix as above. This can be served immediately. **Calories per serving 122**

pomegranate & ginger slice

Calories per serving **121**
Cuts into **20**
Preparation time **25 minutes**
Cooking time **50 minutes**

1½ cups **all-purpose flour**
1 teaspoon **baking soda**
scant ½ cup **milk**
1 **egg**
½ cup firmly packed **dark brown sugar**
⅓ cup **molasses**
5 tablespoons **unsalted butter**
3 pieces of **stem ginger in syrup**, chopped

For the topping
1¼ cups **pomegranate juice**
2 tablespoons **honey**
1 **pomegranate**

Sift the flour and baking soda into a bowl. Beat together the milk and egg in another bowl. Put the sugar, molasses, and butter in a saucepan and heat gently until the butter melts and the sugar dissolves. Remove from the heat and add to the milk mixture with the chopped ginger. Add to the dry ingredients and stir together using a large metal spoon until well combined.

Spoon the mixture into 2 greased and lined 2 lb or 5¼ cup loaf pans and level the surface. Bake in a preheated oven, at 325°F, for 30 minutes or until just firm to the touch and a toothpick inserted into the center comes out clean. Let cool in the pans, then loosen at the ends and transfer to a wire rack. Peel off the lining paper.

Make the topping. Pour the pomegranate juice into a saucepan and bring to a boil, then boil for about 15 minutes, until thick and syrupy and reduced to about 3 tablespoons. Stir in the honey. Halve the pomegranate and push the halves inside out to release the fleshy seeds, discarding any white membrane. Sprinkle the seeds over the top of the cakes. Drizzle with the syrup and cut into small squares to serve.

For raisin & lemon gingerbread, make the cakes as above, reducing the milk to 5 tablespoons and sprinkling ½ cup golden raisins over the mixture in the pans. For the icing, mix together ¾ cup sifted confectioners' sugar and 2 teaspoons lemon juice in a bowl to make a smooth, spoonable icing, then drizzle in lines over the cooled cakes. **Calories per serving 146**

chocolate florentines

Calories per serving **126**
Makes **26**
Preparation time **30 minutes**
Cooking time **15–20 minutes**

7 tablespoons **butter**
½ cup **superfine sugar**
⅓ cup multicolored **candied cherries**, coarsely chopped
¾ cup **sliced almonds**
⅓ cup finely chopped **candied peel**
⅓ cup **hazelnuts**, coarsely chopped
2 tablespoons **all-purpose flour**
5 oz **semisweet chocolate**, broken into pieces

Put the butter and sugar in a saucepan and heat gently until the butter has melted and the sugar dissolved. Remove the pan from the heat and stir in all the remaining ingredients except the chocolate.

Spoon tablespoons of the mixture, well spaced apart, onto 3 baking sheets lined with nonstick parchment paper. Flatten the mounds slightly. Cook one baking sheet at a time in the center of a preheated oven, at 350°F, for 5–7 minutes, until the nuts are golden.

After removing each baking sheet from the oven, neaten and shape the cooked cookies by placing a slightly larger plain round cookie cutter over the top and rotating to smooth and tidy up the edges. Let cool.

Melt the chocolate in a heatproof bowl set over a saucepan of gently simmering water. Peel the cookies off the lining paper and arrange upside down on a wire rack. Spoon the melted chocolate over the flat underside of the cookies and spread the surfaces level. Let cool and harden.

For white chocolate & ginger florentines, add 2 tablespoons ready-chopped candied ginger to the candied fruit and nut mixture. Spread the cooked cookies with melted white chocolate instead of semisweet chocolate as above. **Calories per serving 125**

passion fruit panna cotta

Calories per serving **127**

Serves **4**

Preparation time **20 minutes**, plus setting

2 **gelatin leaves**

8 **passion fruit**

¾ cup **reduced-fat sour cream**

½ cup **fat-free Greek yogurt**

1 teaspoon **superfine sugar**

vanilla bean, split

Soften the gelatin leaves in cold water. Halve the passion fruit and remove the seeds, working over a bowl to catch as much juice as you can. Reserve the seeds for decoration.

Combine the reduced-fat sour cream, yogurt, and passion fruit juice.

Put ½ cup water in a small saucepan, add the sugar and the seeds from the vanilla bean and heat gently, stirring until the sugar has dissolved. Drain the gelatin and add to the pan. Stir until dissolved, then let cool to room temperature.

Mix the gelatin mixture into the sour cream, then pour into 4 ramekins or molds. Refrigerate for 6 hours or until set.

Turn the panna cotta out of their molds by briefly immersing each ramekin in very hot water. Spoon over the reserved seeds to decorate.

For coffee panna cotta, substitute 2 teaspoons strong coffee for the passion fruit and continue as for the recipe, using the vanilla bean. Decorate each panna cotta with chocolate coffee beans, if desired. **Calories per serving 105**

mint granita

Calories per serving **136**
Serves **6**
Preparation time **20 minutes**,
  plus cooling and freezing
Cooking time **4 minutes**

1 cup **superfine sugar**
1¼ cups **water**, plus extra to
  top up
pared zest and juice of 3
  lemons
⅓ cup **fresh mint**, plus
  a few sprigs to decorate
confectioners' sugar, for
  dusting

Put the sugar and measured water into a saucepan,
add the lemon zest and gently heat until the sugar has
dissolved. Increase the heat and boil for 2 minutes.

Tear the tips off the mint stems and finely chop to give
about 3 tablespoons, then reserve. Add the larger mint
leaves and stems to the hot syrup and leave for 1 hour
to cool and for the flavors to develop.

Strain the syrup into a pitcher, add the chopped mint
and lemon juice and top up to 2½ cups with extra cold
water. Pour into a small roasting pan and freeze the
mixture for 2–3 hours or until mushy.

Break up the ice crystals with a fork, then return to
the freezer for 2–3 more hours, breaking up with a
fork once or twice until the mixture is the consistency
of crushed ice. Serve now, spooned into small glass
tumblers, decorated with tiny sprigs of mint dusted
with confectioners' sugar, or leave in the freezer until
required. If leaving in the freezer, allow to soften for
15 minutes before serving. If frozen overnight or longer,
break up with a fork before serving.

For iced ruby grapefruit granita, make a plain sugar
syrup as above, omitting the lemon zest. When cool,
halve 4 ruby grapefruits, squeeze the juice and reserve
4 halved shells. Strain the juice into the syrup instead of
the lemon juice, then freeze as above. Serve the dessert
spooned into the reserved grapefruit shells. **Calories
per serving 143**

cardamom & orange cookies

Calories per serving **153**

Makes about **12**

Preparation time **15 minutes**, plus chilling

Cooking time **15 minutes**

12 **cardamom pods**

1¼ cups **all-purpose flour**

7 tablespoons **slightly salted butter**, chilled and diced

½ cup **confectioners' sugar**, sifted

1 **egg yolk**

finely grated zest of 1 **orange**

For the icing

¾ cup **confectioners' sugar**, sifted

1 tablespoon **orange juice**

Crush the cardamom pods using a mortar and pestle or a small bowl and the end of a rolling pin. Discard the shells and crush the seeds as finely as possible.

Put the flour and crushed seeds in a bowl or food processor. Add the butter and blend with the fingertips or process until the mixture resembles coarse bread crumbs. Add the confectioners' sugar and stir in or blend briefly. Add the egg yolk and orange zest and mix or blend to a dough. Wrap in plastic wrap and chill for 1 hour.

Roll out the dough on a lightly floured surface to ¼ inch thick. Cut out about 12 heart shapes using a 2–2½ inch heart cookie cutter, rerolling the trimmings to make more. Place slightly apart on a large greased baking sheet and bake in a preheated oven, at 375°F, for about 15 minutes, until pale golden. Transfer to a wire rack to cool.

Make the icing. Beat together the confectioners' sugar and orange juice in a bowl to make a smooth, thin icing. Drizzle lines of icing over the cookies to decorate.

For vanilla dessert cookies, make and chill the dough as above, omitting the cardamom and replacing the orange zest with 1 teaspoon vanilla bean paste or extract. Roll out as above and cut out about 12 circles using a 2–2½ inch plain cookie cutter. Bake as above and serve lightly dusted with sifted confectioners' sugar. **Calories per serving 134**

green fruit salad

Calories per serving **167**
Serves **6**
Preparation time **15 minutes**

1 ½ cups **seedless green grapes**, halved
4 **kiwifruits**, peeled, quartered, and sliced
2 **ripe pears**, peeled, cored, and sliced
4 **passion fruits**, halved
¼ cup concentrated **elderflower cordial**
¼ cup **water**
1 ¼ cups **Greek yogurt**
2 tablespoons **honey**

Put the grapes, kiwifruits, and pears in a bowl. Using a teaspoon, scoop the seeds from 3 of the passion fruits into the bowl. Mix 2 tablespoons of the cordial with the measured water and drizzle over the salad. Gently toss together and spoon into 6 glass tumblers.

Stir the remaining undiluted cordial into the yogurt, then mix in the honey. Spoon into the glasses.

Decorate with the remaining passion fruit seeds and serve.

For ruby fruit salad, mix 1 ½ cups halved seedless red grapes with 1 ¼ cups fresh raspberries and 1 cup sliced strawberries. Sprinkle with the seeds from ½ pomegranate, then drizzle with 6 tablespoons red grape juice. Mix the yogurt with honey only, then spoon over the fruit salad. Decorate with a few extra pomegranate seeds. **Calories per serving 123**

creamy mango & passion fruit

Calories per serving **168**
  (plus 46 calories for cookies)
Serves **4**
Preparation time **10 minutes**

1 large **mango**, peeled, pitted,
  and cut into chunks
3 cups **fat-free plain yogurt**
1–2 tablespoons **agave
  nectar**, to taste
1 **vanilla bean**, split in half
  lengthwise
4 **passion fruit**, halved

Place the mango in a food processor or blender and blend to a puree.

Put the yogurt and agave nectar, according to taste, in a large bowl, scrape in the seeds from the vanilla bean and beat together. Gently fold in the mango puree and spoon into tall glasses or glass serving dishes.

Scoop the seeds from the passion fruit and spoon over the mango yogurt. Serve immediately, with 2 thin cookies, if desired.

For black currant & almond yogurt, puree 2 cups black currants as above and fold into the yogurt with the agave nectar, according to taste, and 1 teaspoon almond extract. Spoon into tall serving glasses and sprinkle with toasted almonds, to serve. **Calories per serving 173**

grilled fruits with palm sugar

Calories per serving **176**
Serves **4**
Preparation time **10 minutes**
Cooking time **6–16 minutes**

2 tablespoons **palm sugar**
grated zest and juice of
   1 lime
2 tablespoons **water**
½ teaspoon **cracked black**
   peppercorns
1 lb mixed prepared fruits,
   such as **pineapple** or **peach**
   slices or **mango** wedges

To serve
cinnamon or **vanilla ice**
   cream
lime slices

Put the sugar, lime zest and juice, measured water, and peppercorns in a small saucepan and heat over low heat until the sugar has dissolved. Plunge the base of the pan into ice water to cool.

Brush the cooled syrup over the prepared fruits and cook under a preheated hot broiler for 6–8 minutes on each side, or over a preheated hot gas barbecue or the hot coals of a charcoal barbecue, for 3–4 minutes on each side, until charred and tender.

Serve with scoops of cinnamon or vanilla ice cream and lime slices.

For grilled fruit kebabs, cut the prepared fruits into large chunks, thread onto wooden skewers, presoaked in cold water for 30 minutes, and brush with the cooled syrup before cooking as in the recipe above. **Calories per serving 176**

raspberry shortbread mess

Calories per serving **177**
Serves **4**
Preparation time **5 minutes**

2½ cups **raspberries**, roughly
   chopped
4 **shortbread cookies**,
   roughly crushed
1⅔ cups **fat-free fromage
   frais** or **plain yogurt**
2 tablespoons **confectioners'
   sugar** or **artificial
   sweetener**

Reserving a few raspberries for decoration, combine all
the ingredients in a bowl. Spoon into 4 serving dishes.

Serve immediately, decorated with the reserved
raspberries.

For Eton mess, use 4 meringue nests and 2 cups
strawberries. Hull and halve or quarter the strawberries,
then add them to the fromage frais with the sugar or
sweetener. Break the meringues into chunks and fold
them through the fromage frais, then pile into glasses
and serve. **Calories per serving 143**

frozen fruity yogurt

Calories per serving **194**

Serves **4**

Preparation time **15 minutes**, plus freezing

2½ cups fresh or frozen **raspberries**

3 **nectarines**, skinned, pitted, and chopped

2 tablespoons **confectioners' sugar**

1⅔ cups **Greek yogurt**

¾ cup **low-fat Greek yogurt**

Put half the raspberries and nectarines in a food processor or blender and process until smooth.

Stir the puree and the rest of the fruit into the remaining ingredients, then transfer to a freezerproof container and freeze for 1 hour. Stir well, then return to the freezer and freeze until solid.

Serve the frozen yogurt in scoops, as you would ice cream. It will keep for up to 1 month in the freezer.

For frozen strawberry yogurt, gently cook 1½ cups hulled and chopped strawberries in 2 tablespoons red grape juice. Strain and stir the juice into 1 tablespoon crème de cassis, 2 tablespoons confectioners' sugar, and 1¼ cups plain yogurt, then transfer to a freezerproof container. Continue as above. **Calories per serving 140**

strawberries & meringue

Calories per serving **197**
Serves **4**
Preparation time **15 minutes**
Cooking time **2½ hours**

3 **egg whites**
⅔ cup firmly packed **light brown sugar**
3 teaspoons **cornstarch**
1 teaspoon **white vinegar**
1 teaspoon **vanilla extract**
1½ cups **strawberries**, hulled and sliced

Line 4 individual tart pans or ramekins with nonstick parchment paper. Beat the egg whites until they form stiff peaks, then beat in the sugar, a spoonful at a time, making sure the sugar is incorporated between additions.

Fold in the cornstarch, vinegar, and vanilla extract.

Spoon the mixture into the tart pans or ramekins and cook in a preheated oven, at 250°F, for 2½ hours.

Place the strawberries in an ovenproof dish and bake with the meringues for the last hour of the cooking time.

Spoon the strawberries and any cooking juices over the meringues to serve.

For baked nectarines with orange meringues, add the grated zest of 1 orange to the meringue with the cornstarch. Cut 2 peeled and pitted nectarines into thin slices and place in an ovenproof dish. Sprinkle with 2 tablespoons sugar and 1 tablespoon orange juice, then bake for 45 minutes with the meringues. Serve the fruit on the meringues. **Calories per serving 233**

recipes
under 300
calories

cherry & cinnamon parfait

Calories per serving **201**

Serves **4**

Preparation time **10 minutes**, plus freezing

Cooking time **5 minutes**

11½ oz jar **morello cherries** in syrup

pinch of **ground cinnamon**

½ teaspoon **vanilla extract**

1 tablespoon **sugar**

1 **egg yolk**

⅔ cup **reduced-fat sour cream**

4 **meringue nests**, broken into pieces

fresh cherries, to decorate

Drain the cherries and put 6 tablespoons of the syrup into a small saucepan. Stir the cinnamon, vanilla extract, and sugar into the syrup and heat for 5 minutes or until the sugar has dissolved. Set aside to cool.

Stir the egg yolk through the reduced-fat sour cream. Add the drained cherries to the syrup, then mix in the sour cream and egg. Fold the meringue nests carefully through the mixture.

Transfer to a 1¼ cup freezerproof container and freeze for at least 4 hours. Eat within a day, when the parfait will be softly frozen. Decorate with fresh cherries before serving.

For pineapple parfait, omit the morello cherries and instead drain and chop a 13 oz can sliced pineapple, adding to the syrup as above. Omit the egg yolk, and combine the pineapple, syrup, and reduced-fat sour cream. Fold through the meringue nests. **Calories per serving 180**

sticky toffee & date squares

Calories per serving **201**

Makes **24** squares

Preparation time **25 minutes**, plus cooling

Cooking time **55 minutes**

1¾ sticks **lightly salted butter,** softened, plus extra for greasing

1⅓ cups **pitted dates**, chopped

⅔ cup **water**

⅔ cup **heavy cream**

⅔ cup firmly packed **light brown sugar**

½ cup **superfine sugar**

2 teaspoons **vanilla bean paste**

3 **eggs**

1⅓ cups **all-purpose flour**

2 teaspoons **baking powder**

Grease an 11 x 7 inch shallow baking pan and line with nonstick parchment paper. Put ¾ cup of the dates in a saucepan with the measured water and bring to a boil. Reduce the heat and cook gently for 5 minutes or until the dates are pulpy. Turn into a bowl and let cool. Put the cream, brown sugar, and 5 tablespoons of the butter in a small saucepan and heat gently until the sugar dissolves. Bring to a boil and boil for 5 minutes or until thickened and caramelized. Let cool.

Put the remaining butter in a bowl with the superfine sugar, vanilla bean paste, and eggs, sift in the flour and baking powder and beat with a handheld electric mixer until pale and creamy. Beat in the cooked dates and 6 tablespoons of the caramel mixture. Turn into the pan and level the surface. Sprinkle with the remaining dates.

Bake in a preheated oven, at 350°F, for 25 minutes or until just firm. Spoon the remaining caramel on top and return to the oven for 15 minutes, until the caramel has firmed. Transfer to a wire rack.

For cider-glazed apple slice, grease the pan as above. Put 1½ sticks softened butter, generous ¾ cup unrefined superfine sugar, 1½ cups sifted all-purpose flour, 2 teaspoons baking powder, 1 teaspoon ground pumpkin pie spice, and 3 eggs in a bowl and beat with a handheld electric mixer until smooth and creamy. Stir in ⅓ cup golden raisins and spread in the pan. Core and slice 2 small red apples and sprinkle over the surface. Bake as above for 40 minutes or until just firm. Put ½ cup hard cider in a saucepan and heat until reduced to about 1 tablespoon. Cool and mix with ¾ cup sifted confectioners' sugar until smooth. Drizzle over the cake. **Calories per serving 150**

mango & passion fruit brûlée

Calories per serving **202**

Serves **4**

Preparation time **10 minutes**,
plus chilling

Cooking time **2 minutes**

1 **small mango**, peeled,
pitted, and thinly sliced

2 **passion fruit**, flesh scooped
out

1¼ cups **low-fat plain yogurt**

generous ¾ cup **reduced-fat
sour cream**

1 tablespoon **confectioners'
sugar**

few drops **vanilla extract**

2 tablespoons **Demerara
sugar**

Arrange the mango slices in 4 ramekins.

Stir together the passion fruit flesh, yogurt, sour cream, confectioners' sugar, and vanilla extract in a bowl, then spoon the mixture over the mango. Tap each ramekin to level the surface.

Sprinkle over the Demerara sugar and cook the brûlées under a preheated hot broiler for 1–2 minutes, until the sugar has melted. Chill for about 30 minutes, then serve.

For plum & peach brûlée, replace the mango with 2 sliced peaches. Continue as above, replacing the passion fruit with 4 firm but ripe chopped plums. Before broiling, top each ramekin with a piece of chopped crystallized ginger. **Calories per serving 192**

chocolate brownies

Calories per serving **204**
Makes **9**
Preparation time **10 minutes**
Cooking time **30 minutes**

½ cup **reduced-fat sunflower spread**

2 **eggs**

½ cup firmly packed **light brown sugar**

⅔ cup **all-purpose flour**

⅔ teaspoon **baking powder**

½ cup **unsweetened cocoa powder**, sifted, plus extra to decorate

2 oz **semisweet chocolate**, chopped

1 teaspoon **chocolate extract**

salt

Grease and line a 7 inch square deep cake pan.

Beat together the sunflower spread, eggs, and sugar. Stir in the flour and cocoa, then add the chocolate and chocolate extract. Stir in 1 teaspoon boiling water and a pinch of salt.

Transfer the mixture to the prepared pan and bake in a preheated oven, at 375°F, for 30 minutes or until a toothpick comes out clean when inserted in the center. Let cool in the pan, then cut into 9 squares. Dust with a little cocoa powder to serve.

For rum & raisin sauce, to go with the brownies, gently heat 1 ¼ cups milk in a saucepan with 2 tablespoons cornstarch, 4 tablespoons rum, and 4 tablespoons raisins. Add 2 tablespoons sugar to taste, before pouring the sauce over the cooled brownies. **Calories per serving 54**

strawberry & lavender crush

Calories per serving **208**

Serves **6**

Preparation time **10 minutes**

2½ cups **fresh strawberries**

2 tablespoons **confectioners'
sugar**, plus extra for dusting

4–5 **lavender flower stems**,
plus extra to decorate

1⅔ cups **Greek-style full-fat
yogurt**

6 ready-made **meringue
nests**

Reserve 4 small strawberries for decoration. Hull the remainder, put in a bowl with the confectioners' sugar and mash together with a fork. Alternatively, process the strawberries and confectioners' sugar in a food processor or blender to a smooth puree. Pull off the lavender flowers from the stems and crumble them into the puree to taste.

Put the yogurt in a bowl, crumble in the meringues, then lightly mix together. Add the strawberry puree and fold together with a spoon until marbled. Spoon into 4 dessert glasses.

Cut the reserved strawberries in half, then use together with the lavender flowers to decorate the desserts. Lightly dust with confectioners' sugar and serve immediately.

For peach & rose water crush, peel, halve, and pit 3 peaches, then roughly chop and mash or process in a food processor or blender with 2 tablespoons honey and 2 teaspoons rose water. Continue with the recipe as above, but decorate the desserts with crystallized rose petals. **Calories per serving 227**

banoffee mousse

Calories per serving **209**
Serves **4**
Preparation time **10 minutes**,
  plus setting

2 **gelatin leaves**
3 tablespoons **dulce de leche**
  or **toffee sauce**
½ cup **reduced-fat sour**
  cream
½ cup **honey-dipped banana**
  chips
4 **egg whites**

Soften the gelatin in cold water for 2 minutes.

Put the toffee sauce in a small saucepan over gentle heat and stir in the gelatin until it has dissolved.

Stir the toffee mixture into the reduced-fat sour cream. Chop the dried banana chips, reserving a few whole ones for decoration, and add to the toffee mixture. Meanwhile, beat the egg whites until stiff, then fold through the toffee and banana mixture. Spoon into 4 glasses and decorate with the reserved banana chips and an extra dollop of toffee sauce, if you desire.

For banana & hazelnut toffee creams, mash 2 fresh bananas and mix with the toffee sauce and reduced-fat sour cream, omitting the gelatin and egg whites. Serve topped with ⅓ cup chopped toasted hazelnuts. **Calories per serving 235**

chocolate & nectarine cake

Calories per serving **209**
Serves **6**
Preparation time **15 minutes**
Cooking time **45 minutes**

3 **nectarines**
3 oz **semisweet chocolate**,
  chopped
2 tablespoons **unsalted**
  butter
2 **egg yolks**
⅓ cup **superfine sugar**
½ teaspoon **chocolate extract**
4 **egg whites**
unsweetened cocoa powder,
  for dusting

Grease a 10 inch cake pan and line with parchment paper. Put the nectarines in a bowl and pour over boiling water. Let stand for 1 minute, then peel off the skins. Halve the nectarines and remove the pits. Drain them well on paper towels and arrange, cut side down, in the prepared cake pan.

Put the chocolate and butter in a heatproof bowl and melt together over a pan of simmering water.

Beat together the egg yolks and sugar until the whisk leaves a trail when lifted. The mix should be very pale and quite stiff. Stir in the melted chocolate mixture and chocolate extract.

Beat the egg whites until softly peaking. Stir a spoonful into the cake batter, then fold in the remainder. Spoon the batter over the nectarines.

Bake the cake in a preheated oven, at 350°F, for 45 minutes or until a toothpick inserted comes out clean. Serve warm or cold, dusted with cocoa powder.

For pear & chocolate soufflé cake, make a syrup by bringing ⅔ cup sugar to a boil in 1 cup water. Peel 3 pears and poach them in the syrup for 30 minutes at a gentle simmer. Drain the pears, reserving the syrup, then halve, core, and drain well. Use these instead of the nectarines in the cake as described above. Add the grated zest of 1 orange to the syrup and boil for 2 minutes, then serve with the cake. **Calories per serving 249**

baby banana & peach strudels

Calories per serving **212**
Makes **8**
Preparation time **30 minutes**
Cooking time **15–18 minutes**

2 **bananas**, about 6 oz each
  with skin on, peeled and
  chopped
2 tablespoons **fresh lemon
  juice**
2 small **ripe peaches**, about
  3½ oz each, halved, pitted,
  and sliced
1 cup **blueberries**
2 tablespoons **sugar**
2 tablespoons **fresh bread
  crumbs**
½ teaspoon **ground
  cinnamon**
6 **phyllo pastry sheets**,
  defrosted if frozen
3½ tablespoons **butter**,
  melted
sifted **confectioners' sugar**,
  for dusting

Toss the bananas in the lemon juice, then place in a
large bowl with the peach slices and blueberries. Mix
the sugar, bread crumbs, and cinnamon in a small bowl,
then gently mix with the fruit.

Unfold the pastry sheets and put one in front of you
with the longest edge nearest you.

Cut in half to make 2 rectangles, 9 x 10 inches. Put
2 heaping spoonfuls of the fruit mixture on each, then
fold in the sides, brush the pastry with a little of the
melted butter, and roll up like a parcel. Repeat to make
8 mini strudels using 4 sheets of pastry.

Brush the strudels with a little more melted butter.
Cut the remaining pastry sheets into wide strips, then
wrap them like bandages around the strudels, covering
any tears or splits in the pastry. Place on an ungreased
baking sheet and brush with the remaining butter.

Bake in a preheated oven, at 375°F, for 15–18 minutes
until golden brown and crisp. Let cool on the baking
sheet, then dust with a little sifted confectioners' sugar
and arrange on a serving plate. These are best eaten
on the day they are made.

For traditional apple strudels, replace the bananas
and peaches with 1 lb cored, peeled, and sliced cooking
apples tossed with 2 tablespoons lemon juice and mixed
with ⅓ cup golden raisins. Use ground almonds instead
of the bread crumbs and combine with the cinnamon.
Increase the quantity of sugar to ¼ cup and continue the
recipe as above. **Calories per serving 232**

very berry muffins

Calories per serving **214**
Makes **12**
Preparation time **15 minutes**
Cooking time **25 minutes**

2 cups **all-purpose flour**
4 tablespoons **superfine sugar**
1 tablespoon **baking powder**
1 **egg**, beaten
generous ¾ cup **milk**
3 tablespoons **vegetable oil**
2 cups **mixed berries**, roughly chopped

Mix together all the ingredients, except the berries, to make a smooth batter. Fold in the berries.

Line a 12-cup muffin pan with nonstick paper liners and spoon the batter into the liners. Bake in a preheated oven, at 350°F, for 25 minutes or until a toothpick comes out clean when inserted. Transfer to a wire rack to cool.

For banana & pecan muffins, use 1 cup chopped fresh banana instead of the berries, adding ⅔ cup chopped pecan nuts with the bananas. Select firm but ripe bananas. Serve warm, drizzled with maple syrup, if desired. **Calories per serving 337** (not including maple syrup)

litchi & coconut sherbet

Calories per serving **216**
Serves **6**
Preparation time **30 minutes**,
  plus freezing
Cooking time **2–4 minutes**

14 oz can **pitted litchis** in
  light syrup
¼ cup **superfine sugar**
1²/₃ cups **full-fat coconut
  milk**
grated zest and juice of **1 lime**,
  plus extra pared lime zest, to
  decorate (optional)
chocolate cups (see below),
  to serve (optional)
3 **kiwifruits**, peeled and cut
  into wedges, to decorate

Drain the syrup from the can of litchis into a saucepan,
add the sugar, and heat gently until the sugar has
dissolved. Boil for 2 minutes, then take off the heat
and let cool.

Puree the litchis in a food processor or blender until
smooth, or rub through a sieve. Mix with the coconut
milk, lime zest and juice. Stir in the sugar syrup when
it is cool.

Pour into a shallow plastic container and freeze for
4 hours or until mushy. Beat with a fork or blend in a
food processor or blender until smooth. Pour back into
the plastic container and freeze for 4 hours or overnight
until solid. (Alternatively, freeze in an electric ice-cream
machine for 20 minutes, then transfer to a plastic box
and freeze until required.)

Allow to soften for 15 minutes at room temperature
before serving, then scoop into dishes or chocolate
cups (see below) and decorate with kiwifruit wedges
and pared lime zest curls, if desired.

For chocolate cups, to serve the sherbet in, melt
5 oz semisweet chocolate over a pan of simmering
water, then divide between 4 squares of nonstick
parchment paper and spread into rough-shaped
circles about 6 inches in diameter. Drape the paper
over upturned glass tumblers, with the chocolate
uppermost, so that the paper falls in soft folds.
Chill until set, then lift the paper and chocolate off
the tumblers, turn over and carefully ease the paper
away. **Calories per serving 145**

pistachio & chocolate meringues

Calories per serving **217**
Makes **12**
Preparation time **30 minutes**
Cooking time **45–60 minutes**

3 **egg whites**
generous ¾ cup **superfine sugar**
½ cup **shelled pistachio nuts**, finely chopped
5 oz **semisweet chocolate**, broken into pieces
⅔ cup **heavy cream**

Whisk the egg whites in a large clean bowl until stiff. Gradually whisk in the sugar, a teaspoonful at a time, until it has all been added. Whisk for a few minutes more until the meringue mixture is thick and glossy.

Fold in the pistachios, then spoon heaping teaspoonfuls of the mixture into rough swirly mounds on 2 large baking sheets lined with nonstick parchment paper.

Bake in a preheated oven, at 225°F, for 45–60 minutes or until the meringues are firm and may be easily peeled off the paper. Let cool still on the paper.

Melt the chocolate in a heatproof bowl set over a saucepan of gently simmering water. Lift the meringues off the paper and dip the bases into the chocolate. Return to the paper, tilted on their sides and leave in a cool place until the chocolate has hardened.

To serve, whip the cream until just holding its shape then use to sandwich the meringues together in pairs. Arrange in paper cake liners, if desired, on a cake plate or stand. Eat on the day they are filled. (Left plain, the meringues will keep for 2–3 days.)

For saffron & chocolate meringues, add a large pinch of saffron threads to the egg whites when first whisking them and omit the pistachios. Dip the meringues in the melted chocolate, fill with the whipped cream, and serve as above. **Calories per serving 192**

mango & kiwi upside down cakes

Calories per serving **218**
Cuts into **18**
Preparation time **30 minutes**
Cooking time **30–35 minutes**

1 large **mango**
4 tablespoons **apricot jelly**
grated zest and juice of 2
   limes
2 **kiwifruit**, sliced
1 cup **soft margarine**
²/₃ cup **superfine sugar**
½ cup firmly packed **light
   brown sugar**
2 cups **all-purpose flour**
2 teaspoons **baking powder**
4 **eggs**

Cut a thick slice off each side of the mango to reveal the large flat central pit. Cut the flesh away from the pit, then peel and slice.

Mix the apricot jelly with the juice of 1 of the limes, then spoon into the bottom of a 7 x 11 inch roasting pan lined with nonstick parchment paper. Arrange the mango and kiwifruit randomly over the top.

Put the lime zest and the rest of the juice in a mixing bowl or a food processor, add the remaining ingredients, and beat until smooth. Spoon over the top of the fruit and spread the surface level. Bake in a preheated oven, at 350°F, for 30–35 minutes, until the cake is well risen, golden, and springs back when gently pressed with a fingertip.

Leave to cool in the pan for 10 minutes, then invert the pan onto a wire rack, remove the pan and lining paper and let cool completely. Cut into 18 pieces and serve warm with whipped cream. This is best eaten on the day it is made.

For apricot & cranberry upside down cakes, spoon cranberry sauce over the base of the pan instead of the apricot jelly. Cover with a 14 oz can apricot halves, drained and arranged in rows, instead of the fresh fruit. Replace the lime zest and juice from the cake mixture with the grated zest of 1 orange. Top the fruit with the cake batter and bake as above. **Calories per serving 208**

very berry fool

Calories per serving **219**

Serves **4**

Preparation time **5 minutes**,
  plus cooling and chilling

Cooking time **about
  5 minutes**

3 tablespoons **crème de
  cassis** or **spiced red fruit
  cordial**

2 cups **mixed frozen berries**

2–4 tablespoons **confectioners'
  sugar**, to taste

2 cups **fat-free fromage frais**
  or **plain yogurt**

1 cup **low-fat black currant
  yogurt**

1 **vanilla bean**, split in half
  lengthwise

toasted **sliced almonds**, to
  serve

Put the crème de cassis or cordial in a saucepan over low heat and gently heat, then add the berries. Stir, cover, and cook for about 5 minutes or until the fruit has thawed and is beginning to collapse. Remove from the heat and stir in 1–3 tablespoons of the confectioners' sugar, according to taste. Cool completely, then chill for at least 1 hour.

Mix together the fromage frais, yogurt, and 1 tablespoon of the confectioners' sugar in a bowl. Scrape in the seeds from the vanilla bean and beat to combine.

Fold the berries into the fromage frais mixture until just combined. Carefully spoon into decorative glasses or glass serving dishes and serve immediately, sprinkled with toasted almonds, if desired.

For exotic fruit fool, replace the crème de cassis with 3 tablespoons coconut cream and the mixed berries with 8 oz exotic fruit mix and add 1 tablespoon lime juice. Heat as above, then blend in a food processor or blender until smooth. Chill as above. Mix the fromage frais with 2 tablespoons coconut cream and 1 cup fat-free mango yogurt instead of the black currant yogurt. Fold in the fruit puree and serve sprinkled with toasted coconut flakes. **Calories per serving 262**

griddled bananas with blueberries

Calories per serving **220**
Serves **4**
Preparation time **5 minutes**
Cooking time **8–10 minutes**

4 **bananas**, unpeeled
8 tablespoons **fat-free Greek yogurt**
4 tablespoons **steel-cut** or **rolled oats**
1 cup **blueberries**
honey, to serve

Heat a ridged grill pan over medium-hot heat, add the bananas, and grill for 8–10 minutes or until the skins are beginning to blacken, turning occasionally.

Transfer the bananas to serving dishes and, using a sharp knife, cut open lengthwise. Spoon over the yogurt and sprinkle with the oats and blueberries. Serve immediately, drizzled with 1 teaspoon honey per banana.

For oat, ginger & raisin yogurt, mix ½ teaspoon ground ginger with the yogurt in a bowl. Sprinkle with 2–4 tablespoons dark brown sugar, according to taste, the oats, and 4 tablespoons golden raisins. Let stand for 5 minutes before serving. **Calories per serving 208**

gluten-free banoffee bites

Calories per serving **222**
Makes **10**
Preparation time **10 minutes**,
    plus cooling
Cooking time **12 minutes**

1 ¼ cups **brown rice flour**
5 tablespoons **lightly salted
    butter**, softened
⅓ cup **unrefined superfine
    sugar**
2 teaspoons **gluten-free
    baking powder**
1 **large banana**, mashed
2 **eggs**
6 **toffees**, chopped
1 tablespoon firmly packed
    light brown sugar
2 tablespoons **chewy banana
    slices** or **dried banana
    chips**, to decorate

Line a 12-cup muffin pan with paper liners.

Place the flour, butter, superfine sugar, baking powder, banana, and eggs in a bowl and beat with a handheld electric mixer until smooth. Stir in the toffees. Divide among the liners and sprinkle over most of the brown sugar.

Bake in a preheated oven, at 400°F, for 10–12 minutes, until just firm. Remove the cakes from the oven and transfer to a wire rack to cool.

Top with chewy banana slices or banana chips and sprinkle with the remaining sugar.

For walnut & brown sugar butterflies, make the muffin batter as above, replacing the toffees with ⅓ cup finely chopped walnuts. Bake as above and let cool. Thoroughly beat 7 tablespoons softened unsalted butter in a bowl with ⅔ cup firmly packed light brown sugar until smooth, pale, and creamy. Cut a circle from the center top of each cake using a small sharp knife. Cut each circle in half. Spoon or pipe the buttercream into the centers and position the halved circles to resemble butterfly wings. Dust lightly with confectioners' sugar. **Calories per serving 353**

banoffee meringues

Calories per serving **224**
Makes **8**
Preparation time **30 minutes**
Cooking time **1−1¼ hours**

3 **egg whites**
½ cup firmly packed **light brown sugar**
⅓ cup **superfine sugar**

To decorate
1 **small ripe banana**
1 tablespoon **lemon juice**
⅔ cup **heavy cream**
½ cup store-bought **toffee fudge ice cream sauce**

Whisk the egg whites in a large clean bowl until stiff. Gradually whisk in the sugars, a teaspoonful at a time, until it has all been added. Whisk for a few minutes more until the meringue mixture is thick and glossy.

Using a dessertspoon, take a large scoop of meringue mixture, then scoop off the first spoon using a second spoon and drop onto a large baking sheet lined with nonstick parchment paper to make an oval-shaped meringue. Continue until all the mixture has been used.

Bake in a preheated oven, at 225°F, for 1−1¼ hours or until the meringues are firm and easy to peel off the paper. Leave on the paper to cool.

To serve, roughly mash the banana with the lemon juice. Whip the cream until it forms soft swirls, then beat in 2 tablespoons of the toffee fudge sauce. Combine with the mashed banana, then use to sandwich the meringues together in pairs and arrange in paper cake liners. Drizzle with the remaining toffee fudge sauce and serve immediately. Unfilled meringues may be stored in an airtight container for up to 3 days.

For coffee toffee meringues, make the meringues as above. To make the filling, whip the cream, then stir in 1−2 teaspoons instant espresso powder, dissolved in 1 teaspoon boiling water. Use to sandwich the meringues together in pairs. Drizzle toffee fudge sauce over the top of the meringues. **Calories per serving 209**

apricot tea bread

Calories per serving **230**

Cuts into **10**

Preparation time **25 minutes**,
  plus soaking

Cooking time **1 hour**

$\frac{2}{3}$ cup ready-to-eat **dried
  apricots**, chopped

$\frac{2}{3}$ cup **golden raisins**

$\frac{2}{3}$ cup **raisins**

$\frac{3}{4}$ cup **superfine sugar**

1 $\frac{1}{4}$ cups **hot strong tea**

2 $\frac{1}{4}$ cups **all-purpose flour**

2 $\frac{1}{4}$ teaspoons **baking powder**

1 teaspoon **baking soda**

1 teaspoon **ground cinnamon**

1 **egg**, beaten

Put the dried fruits and sugar in a mixing bowl, add the hot tea and mix together. Let soak for 4 hours or overnight.

Mix the flour, baking powder, baking soda, and cinnamon together, add to the soaked fruit with the beaten egg, and mix together well.

Spoon into a greased 2 lb loaf pan, its bottom and 2 long sides also lined with oiled wax paper. Spread the surface level, then bake in the center of a preheated oven, at 325°F, for about 1 hour, until well risen, the top has cracked, and a toothpick inserted into the center comes out clean.

Let cool in the pan for 10 minutes, then loosen the edges and lift out of the pan using the lining paper. Transfer to a wire rack, peel off the lining paper, and let cool completely. Cut into slices and spread with a little butter to serve. Store, unbuttered, in an airtight container for up to 1 week.

For prune & orange bread, use 1 cup ready-to-eat pitted prunes, chopped, instead of the apricots and golden raisins, and increase the quantity of raisins to $\frac{3}{4}$ cup. Mix with the superfine sugar as above, add the grated zest of 1 orange, then soak in $\frac{2}{3}$ cup orange juice and $\frac{2}{3}$ cup boiling water instead of the tea. Add the flour, baking powder, baking soda, and beaten egg as above, omitting the cinnamon. Spoon into a loaf pan and continue the recipe as above. **Calories per serving 227**

summer fruit crunch

Calories per serving **231**
Serves **4**
Preparation time **10 minutes**
Cooking time **20 minutes**

½ cup **rolled oats**
½ teaspoon **ground cinnamon**
½ teaspoon **pumpkin pie spice**
pinch of **ground ginger**
1 tablespoon **butter**, melted
1 tablespoon **honey**
2 tablespoons **golden raisins**
13 oz mixed fresh or frozen **summer fruits**
½ cup **confectioners' sugar**, plus extra to decorate
2 tablespoons **crème de cassis**
½ teaspoon **vanilla extract**
1 tablespoon **sliced almonds**, toasted, to garnish

Mix the oats and spices with the melted butter and honey until well combined.

Press onto a baking sheet and cook in a preheated oven, at 350°F, for 20 minutes, turning once. Remove and let cool before mixing in the golden raisins.

Meanwhile, put the summer fruits in a saucepan with the confectioners' sugar and 1 tablespoon water. Warm over medium-low heat, stirring occasionally, until the fruit begins to collapse. Remove from the heat and stir in the crème de cassis and vanilla extract.

Spoon the fruit into dishes and sprinkle with the crunchy topping. Decorate with the toasted almonds and a sprinkling of confectioners' sugar. Serve immediately.

For autumn plum crunch, pit and quarter 1 lb plums and use instead of the summer fruits. Cook the plums in ½ cup apple juice until just tender. Substitute the crème de cassis with sloe gin. Spoon into the dishes and finish as above. **Calories per serving 236**

blueberry & lemon ice cream

Calories per serving **234**

Serves **4**

Preparation time **10 minutes**, plus freezing

1 lb **frozen blueberries**

2 cups **fat-free Greek yogurt**

1 cup **confectioners' sugar**, plus extra to decorate

grated zest of 2 **lemons**

1 tablespoon **lemon juice**

Reserve a few blueberries for decoration. Put the remainder of the blueberries in a food processor or blender with the yogurt, confectioners' sugar, and lemon zest and juice and process until smooth.

Spoon the mixture into a 2½ cup freezerproof container and freeze.

Eat when the frozen yogurt is softly frozen and easily spoonable. Before serving, decorate with the reserved blueberries and a sprinkling of confectioners' sugar. Use within 3 days.

For peach & black currant ice cream waffles, lightly toast 4 waffles, then top each with a sliced canned peach and drizzle with honey. Serve with black currant and lemon ice cream. Use 1 lb frozen black currants in place of the blueberries. The same quantity of frozen blackberries or raspberries can also be used. **Calories per serving 366**

sweet carrot & rosemary scones

Calories per serving **236**
Makes **12**
Preparation time **15 minutes**
Cooking time **8–10 minutes**

2 cups **stoneground spelt flour**

2 teaspoons **baking powder**

½ teaspoon **cream of tartar**

2 teaspoons **fresh rosemary**, finely chopped

2 tablespoons **superfine sugar**

3½ tablespoons **slightly salted butter**, chilled and diced

2 cups finely shredded **small carrots**

6 tablespoons **milk**, plus extra to glaze

To serve

mascarpone cheese

fruit jelly, such as crab apple, apple, or orange

Sift the flour, baking powder, and cream of tartar into a bowl or food processor, tipping in the grains left in the sieve. Stir in the rosemary and sugar. Add the butter and blend with the fingertips or process until the mixture resembles bread crumbs. Stir in the shredded carrots and milk and mix or blend briefly to a soft dough, adding a dash more milk if the dough feels dry.

Knead the dough on a lightly floured surface until smooth, then roll out to ¾ inch thick. Cut out 22–24 circles using a 1¼ inch plain cookie cutter, rerolling the trimmings to make more. Place slightly apart on a greased baking sheet and brush with milk.

Bake in a preheated oven, at 425°F, for 8–10 minutes, until risen and pale golden. Transfer to a wire rack to cool.

Split the scones and serve spread with mascarpone and fruit jelly.

For whole-wheat apple & raisin scones, mix 1 cup whole-wheat flour, ¾ cup all-purpose flour, 1 teaspoon ground pumpkin pie spice, and 2 ¾ teaspoons baking powder in a bowl or food processor. Add 3 tablespoons slightly salted butter, chilled and diced, and blend with the fingertips or process until the mixture resembles bread crumbs. Stir or blend in ⅓ cup golden raisins, chopped, and 1 peeled, cored, and grated dessert apple. Add ½ cup milk and mix or blend to a soft dough, adding a little more milk if the dough feels dry. Roll out, shape, and bake as above. **Calories per serving 102**

chocolate yum yums

Calories per serving **240**

Cuts into **12**

Preparation time **15 minutes**,
   plus chilling

5 oz **semisweet chocolate**,
   broken into pieces

½ cup **crunchy peanut butter**

2 tablespoons **butter**

2 tablespoons **light corn
   syrup**

5 oz **graham crackers**

⅓ cup **almonds** or **cashew
   nuts**

candied almonds, coarsely
   chopped, to decorate

Put the chocolate, peanut butter, butter, and syrup in a saucepan and heat gently until melted, stirring occasionally. Remove from the heat.

Place the crackers in a plastic bag and crush coarsely using a rolling pin. Stir the crushed crackers and the nuts into the chocolate and stir until evenly coated.

Spoon the mixture into an 8 inch shallow square cake pan lined with nonstick parchment paper, and spread the surface level. Chill for 4 hours until firm. Lift the cake out of the pan using the lining paper, cut into 12 small squares and peel off the paper. Decorate with candied almonds. Store in an airtight container for up to 3 days.

For chocolate marshmallow wedges, omit the peanut butter, nuts, and candied almonds. Melt the chocolate with 5 tablespoons butter and ¼ cup light corn syrup. Cool slightly, then stir in 2½ oz coarsely chopped ladyfingers, ⅓ cup coarsely chopped candied cherries, and 2 cups mini marshmallows. Spoon into a plastic wrap-lined 8 inch round cake pan and sprinkle the top with ½ cup halved mini marshmallows. Chill as above. Remove from the pan, peel off the plastic wrap, and cut into thin wedges. **Calories per serving 200**

chocolate cornflake bars

Calories per serving **240**

Makes **12**

Preparation time **10 minutes**, plus chilling

Cooking time **3 minutes**

7 oz **milk chocolate**, broken into pieces

2 tablespoons **light corn syrup**

3½ tablespoons **olive oil spread**

4 cups **cornflakes**

Melt the chocolate with the corn syrup and olive oil spread in a bowl over a pan of simmering water.

Stir in the cornflakes and mix well together.

Grease an 11 x 7 inch pan. Turn the mixture into the pan, chill until set, then cut into 12 bars.

For crunchy muesli & apricot cakes, replace the cornflakes with 1¼ cups muesli and ⅓ cup dried apricots, chopped. Combine with the chocolate mixture, spoon into 12 paper cupcake liners and chill until set. **Calories per serving 247**

st clement's cheesecake

Calories per serving **245**
Serves **10**
Preparation time **10 minutes**,
   plus cooling and chilling
Cooking time **50 minutes**

3½ tablespoons **unsalted
   butter**
2 cups crushed **low-fat oat
   cookies**
2 cups **quark** or **low-fat
   cream cheese**
⅔ cup **superfine sugar**
2 **eggs**
grated zest and juice of 2
   oranges
grated zest and juice of 1
   lemon
½ cup **golden raisins**
juliennes of orange and
   lemon zest, to decorate

Lightly grease an 8 inch nonstick, removable-bottomed round cake pan.

Melt the butter in a saucepan, stir in the cookie crumbs, then press them over the bottom and sides of the cake pan. Bake in a preheated oven, at 300°F, for 10 minutes.

Beat together the remaining ingredients in a bowl, spoon the mixture into the cake pan and bake for 40 minutes, until just firm. Turn off the oven and leave the cheesecake to cool in the oven for an hour.

Transfer the cheesecake to the refrigerator for 2 hours, then serve decorated with juliennes of orange and lemon zest.

For lime & raspberry cheesecake, replace the oranges, lemon, and golden raisins with 2–3 drops vanilla extract and the grated zest and juice of 1 lime, then cook as above. Once chilled, decorate with 1 cup raspberries. **Calories per serving 221**

cidered apple & fig loaf

Calories per serving **246**

Cuts into **10**

Preparation time **20 minutes**,
plus soaking

Cooking time **1 hour–1 hour
10 minutes**

1¼ cups **hard cider**

1 **large cooking apple**, about
10 oz in total, cored, peeled,
and chopped

1 cup **ready-to-eat dried figs**,
chopped

⅔ cup **sugar**

2½ cups **all-purpose flour**

2½ teaspoons **baking powder**

2 **eggs**, beaten

1 tablespoon **sunflower
seeds**

1 tablespoon **pumpkin seeds**

Pour the cider into a saucepan, add the apple and figs
and bring to a boil. Simmer for 3–5 minutes until the
apples are just tender but still firm. Remove the pan
from the heat and let soak for 4 hours.

Mix the sugar, flour, baking powder, and eggs into the
soaked fruit and stir well.

Spoon into a greased 2 lb loaf pan, its bottom and
2 long sides also lined with oiled wax paper, and
spread the surface level. Sprinkle with the seeds and
bake in the center of a preheated oven, at 325°F, for
1 hour–1 hour 10 minutes, until well risen, the top has
slightly cracked, and a toothpick inserted into the center
comes out clean.

Let cool in the pan for 10 minutes, then loosen the
edges and lift out of the pan using the lining paper.
Transfer to a wire rack, peel off the lining paper, and
let cool completely. Serve cut into slices and spread
with a little butter. Store in an airtight container for up
to 1 week.

For apple & mixed fruit loaf, cook the apple as
above in 1¼ cups apple juice instead of cider with
1 cup luxury mixed dried fruit instead of dried figs.
Continue as above, spooning the mixture into the pan
and sprinkling the top with coarsely crushed sugar
lumps or leaving plain if preferred. **Calories per
serving 252**

caramelized blueberry custards

Calories per serving **251**

Serves **6**

Preparation time **10 minutes**,
   plus cooling

Cooking time **5 minutes**

¾ cup **granulated sugar**

3 tablespoons **cold water**

2 tablespoons **boiling water**

1¼ cups fresh (not frozen)
   blueberries

1⅔ cups **fromage frais** or
   plain yogurt

½ cup store-bought **custard**

Put the sugar and measured cold water into a skillet and heat gently, stirring very occasionally, until the sugar has completely dissolved. Bring to a boil, then cook for 3–4 minutes, without stirring, until the syrup is just changing color and is golden around the edges.

Add the measured boiling water, standing well back as the syrup will spit, then tilt the pan to mix. Add the blueberries and cook for 1 minute. Remove the skillet from the heat and let cool slightly.

Mix the fromage frais and custard together, spoon into 6 small dishes, then spoon the blueberry mixture over the top. Serve immediately, with baby meringues, if desired.

For banana custards, make the caramel as above, then add 2 sliced bananas instead of the blueberries. Cool slightly, then spoon over the custard and fromage frais mixture. Decorate with grated semisweet chocolate. Calories per serving 286

mini christmas cakes

Calories per serving **253**

Makes **12**

Preparation time **40 minutes**,
   plus cooling

Cooking time **15 minutes**

3½ tablespoons **lightly salted butter**, softened

¼ cup firmly packed **dark brown sugar**

1 **egg**

½ cup **all-purpose flour**

½ teaspoon **ground pumpkin pie spice**

¾ teaspoon **baking powder**

⅓ cup **mixed dried fruit**

2 tablespoons **Brazil nuts**, chopped

2 tablespoons **brandy** or **orange-flavored liqueur**

2 tablespoons **apricot jelly**

1 teaspoon **hot water**

8 oz **marzipan**

confectioners' sugar, for dusting

1½ cups **royal icing sugar**, sifted

edible silver dragées, to decorate

Place 12 mini silicone muffin liners on a baking sheet.

Put the butter, sugar, and egg in a bowl, sift in the flour, pumpkin pie spice, and baking powder and beat with a handheld electric mixer until light and creamy. Beat in the dried fruit and nuts. Divide among the liners.

Bake in a preheated oven, at 350°F, for 15 minutes or until risen and just firm. Leave in the liners for 2 minutes, then transfer to a wire rack to cool completely.

Using a toothpick, pierce holes over the tops of the cakes and spoon over the brandy or orange liqueur. Store in an airtight container for up to 1 week.

Mix the apricot jelly with the measured hot water and brush over the tops of the cakes. Thinly roll out the marzipan on a surface dusted with confectioners' sugar and cut out 1¾ inch circles using a small cutter, rerolling the trimmings to make more. Press onto the tops of the cakes.

Beat the royal icing sugar in a bowl with enough cold water to make a softly peaking consistency. Swirl a little over the cakes and decorate with silver balls.

For Christmas tree cakes, make the cakes as above and cover with marzipan. Thinly roll out 13½ oz green ready-to-use fondant on a surface dusted with confectioners' sugar and cut out 16 simple Christmas tree shapes using a small cutter. Transfer to a tray lined with parchment paper for 2–3 hours to firm up. Spread the cakes with royal icing as above and gently position a tree on top of each. Decorate with garlands of red decorator icing, pushing silver dragées into the piping to secure. **Calories per serving 266**

stollen slice

Calories per serving **253**

Makes **15 slices**

Preparation time **30 minutes**, plus rising

Cooking time **25 minutes**

3 tablespoons **salted butter**, plus extra for greasing

1¼ cups **white bread flour**, plus extra for dusting

1½ teaspoons **active dry yeast**

½ teaspoon **ground pumpkin pie spice**

2 tablespoons **superfine sugar**

scant ½ cup **warm milk**

½ cup **golden raisins**

2½ tablespoons **chopped almonds**

2 tablespoons **chopped candied peel**

5 oz **marzipan**

confectioners' sugar, for dusting

Grease a large loaf pan with a base measurement of about 10 x 4 inches. Put the flour, yeast, pumpkin pie spice, and sugar in a bowl. Melt 2 tablespoons of the butter, mix with the milk, and add to the bowl. Mix with a blunt knife to make a soft but not sticky dough. Turn out onto a lightly floured surface and knead for 10 minutes until smooth and elastic. (Alternatively, use a stand mixer with a dough hook and knead for 5 minutes.) Place in a lightly oiled bowl, cover with plastic wrap, and let rise in a warm place for about 1½ hours or until doubled in size.

Turn the dough out onto a floured surface and knead in the golden raisins, almonds, and candied peel. Cover loosely with a dish towel and let rest for 10 minutes. Roll out the dough on a floured surface to a 10 x 8 inch rectangle. Roll the marzipan under the palms of your hands to form a log shape about 9 inches long and flatten to about ¼ inch thick. Lay the marzipan down the length of the dough, slightly to one side, and fold the rest of the dough over it. Transfer to the pan and press down gently.

Cover loosely with oiled plastic wrap and let rise in a warm place for about 30 minutes until slightly risen. Remove the plastic wrap. Bake in a preheated oven, at 425°F, for 25 minutes until risen and golden. Leave for 5 minutes, then turn out of the pan, place on a wire rack, cover with a sheet of foil, and place a weight on top to keep the stollen compact while cooling. Melt the remaining butter and brush over the bread. Dust generously with confectioners' sugar.

cidered apple jellies

Calories per serving **254**
Preparation time **20 minutes**,
  plus chilling
Cooking time **15 minutes**
Finishing time **5 minutes**
Serves **6**

2 lb **cooking apples**, peeled,
  cored, and sliced
1¼ cups **hard cider**
⅔ cup **water**, plus
  4 tablespoons
⅓ cup **sugar**
finely grated zest of 2 **lemons**
4 teaspoons **powdered
  gelatin**
⅔ cup **heavy cream**

Put the apples, cider, ⅔ cup water, sugar, and the zest of one of the lemons into a saucepan. Cover and simmer for 15 minutes until the apples are soft.

Meanwhile put the 4 tablespoons of water into a small bowl and sprinkle over the gelatin, making sure that all the powder is absorbed by the water. Set aside.

Add the gelatin to the hot apples and stir until completely dissolved. Puree the apple mixture in a blender or food processor until smooth, then pour into 6 tea cups. Allow to cool, then chill for 4–5 hours until fully set.

When ready to serve, whip the cream until it forms soft peaks. Spoon over the jellies and sprinkle with the remaining lemon zest.

For cidered apple granita, omit the gelatin and pour the pureed apple mixture into a shallow dish so that the mixture is about 1 inch deep or less. Freeze for about 2 hours until mushy around the edges, then beat with a fork. Freeze for 2 hours more, beating the granita at 30-minute intervals until the texture of crushed ice. Freeze until ready to serve, then scoop into small glasses. **Calories per serving 250**

tropical ginger cake

Calories per serving **257**
Makes **20** squares
Preparation time **30 minutes**,
  plus cooling
Cooking time **25 minutes**

1¼ sticks plus 1 tablespoon
  butter, plus extra for
  greasing
½ cup firmly packed **light
  brown sugar**
3 tablespoons **light corn
  syrup**
2 cups **all-purpose flour**
3 teaspoons **baking powder**
3 teaspoons **ground ginger**
½ cup **shredded coconut**
3 **eggs**, beaten
7 oz **canned pineapple rings**,
  drained and chopped

Lime frosting
7 tablespoons **unsalted
  butter**, softened
2 cups **confectioners' sugar**,
  sifted
grated zest and juice of **1 lime**

To decorate
ready-to-eat **dried papaya**
  and **apricot**, diced
dried **coconut shavings**

Grease and line the bottom of a 7 x 11 inch roasting pan
with nonstick parchment paper. Heat the butter, sugar,
and syrup gently in a saucepan, stirring until melted.

Mix the dry ingredients together in a mixing bowl, then
stir in the melted butter mixture and beat together until
smooth. Stir in the eggs, then the chopped pineapple.
Turn into the pan and level the surface.

Bake in a preheated oven, at 350°F, for about 20 minutes,
until well risen and firm to touch. Let cool in the pan for
10 minutes, then transfer to a wire rack.

Make the lime frosting by beating the butter,
confectioners' sugar, and half the lime zest and juice
together to make a smooth light mixture. Turn the cake
over so the top is uppermost, then spread with the
frosting. Decorate with a sprinkling of the remaining
lime zest, ready-to-eat dried fruits, and coconut
shavings. Cut into 20 squares to serve.

For ginger muffin slice, grease and line a 1½–2 lb
loaf pan with nonstick parchment paper. Beat together
7 tablespoons melted lightly salted butter, ¾ cup milk,
and 1 egg. Mix together 2 cups all-purpose flour,
2 teaspoons baking powder, 2 teaspoons ground ginger,
¾ cup unrefined superfine sugar, 2 tablespoons
steel-cut oats, and ½ cup raisins in a bowl. Stir in the
milk mixture until just combined and turn into the pan.
Bake in a preheated oven, at 350°F, for about
45 minutes, until risen and just firm. Dust with sugar
and serve freshly baked. **Calories per serving 138**

fig & honey pots

Calories per serving **260**
Serves **4**
Preparation time **10 minutes**,
  plus chilling

6 ripe **fresh figs**, thinly sliced,
  plus 2 extra, cut into wedges,
  to decorate (optional)
2 cups **full-fat Greek yogurt**
4 tablespoons **honey**
2 tablespoons **pistachio nuts**,
  chopped

Arrange the fig slices snugly in the bottom of 4 glasses or glass bowls. Spoon the yogurt over the figs and chill in the refrigerator for 10–15 minutes.

Just before serving, drizzle 1 tablespoon honey over each dessert and sprinkle the pistachio nuts on top. Decorate with the wedges of fig, if desired.

For hot figs with honey, heat a ridged grill pan, add 8 whole ripe fresh figs and cook for 8 minutes, turning occasionally, until charred on the outside. Alternatively, cook under a preheated broiler. Remove and cut in half. Divide among 4 plates, top each with 1 heaping tablespoonful of Greek yogurt, and drizzle with a little clear honey. **Calories per serving 151**

lime & mango sorbet

Calories per serving **260**

Serves **4**

Preparation time **10 minutes**, plus freezing

Cooking time **5 minutes**

¾ cup **sugar**

1 cup **water**

1 cup **lime juice**

grated zest of **1 lime**

3 **mangoes**, peeled and pitted

2 **egg whites**

Line a 2 lb loaf pan with plastic wrap or nonstick parchment paper. Put the sugar in a saucepan, add 1 cup water and warm gently until the sugar is dissolved. Remove from the heat and stir in the lime juice and grated zest.

Meanwhile, process the mango flesh to make a smooth puree, reserving 4 thin slices for the decoration. Stir the puree into the lime syrup and pour the mixture into the loaf pan. Freeze for at least 4 hours or overnight until solid.

Remove the sorbet from the pan and blend or process with the egg whites. Return the mixture to the pan and return to the freezer until firm. Eat within 3 days, because the flavor of fresh fruit sorbet deteriorates quickly and this one has raw egg in it. Before serving, decorate each portion of sorbet with a thin slice of mango and serve with a couple of wafer cookies.

For passion fruit sorbet, omit the mangoes and use 1 cup passion fruit juice instead of the lime juice. The passion fruit juice can be bought or scooped from fresh fruit. To prepare fresh fruit, halve and scoop out the seeds and pulp into a sieve. Rub all the juice through the sieve, then discard the seeds. **Calories per serving 175**

poached apricots with pistachios

Calories per serving **260**
Serves **4**
Preparation time **10 minutes**,
  plus chilling and cooling
Cooking time **8 minutes**

²/₃ cup **sugar**
1 ¼ cups **water**
2 strips of **lemon peel**
2 **cardamom pods**
1 **vanilla bean**
12 **apricots**, halved and pitted
1 tablespoon **lemon juice**
1 tablespoon **rose water**
¼ cup **pistachio nuts**, finely
  chopped
vanilla ice cream or **Greek-
  style yogurt**, to serve
  (optional)

Put a large bowl in the freezer to chill. Put the sugar
and measured water in a wide saucepan and heat over
low heat until the sugar has dissolved. Meanwhile, cut
the lemon peel into fine strips, crush the cardamom
pods, and split the vanilla bean in half. Add the lemon
strips, cardamom, and vanilla bean to the pan.

Add the apricots and simmer gently for 5 minutes or
until softened. Remove from the heat, add the lemon
juice and rose water and transfer to the chilled bowl.
Let cool until required.

Spoon the apricots and a little of the syrup into serving
bowls, sprinkle with the pistachio nuts, and serve with
ice cream or Greek-style yogurt, if you desire.

For poached peaches with almonds, follow the
first stage of the recipe above, but replace the lemon
peel with orange peel and the cardamom pods with
½ cinnamon stick. Peel, halve, and pit 4 large peaches,
then poach until softened and add orange juice and
orange flower water in place of the lemon juice and
rose water. After cooling, serve sprinkled with toasted
sliced almonds instead of the pistachio nuts. **Calories
per serving 151**

citrus refresher

calories per serving **274**

Serves **4**

Preparation time **10 minutes**

Cooking time **6–7 minutes**

⅔ cup **chilled orange juice** from a carton

⅔ cup **water**

⅔ cup **sugar**

juice of ½ **lemon**

2 **ruby grapefruit**

4 **oranges** (a mix of ordinary and blood oranges, if available)

1 **orange-fleshed melon**

½ **pomegranate**

Pour the orange juice and measured water into a saucepan, add the sugar, and heat gently until the sugar has dissolved, then simmer for 5 minutes until syrupy. Take off the heat and mix in the lemon juice.

Cut a slice off the top and bottom of each grapefruit, then cut away the rest of the peel in downward slices using a small serrated knife. Holding the fruit over a bowl, cut between the membranes to release the segments. Cut a slice off the top and bottom of the oranges, then cut away the rest of the peel. Cut into segments and add to the bowl.

Cut the melon in half, scoop out the seeds, then cut away the peel and dice the flesh. Add to the citrus fruit, then pour over the syrup. Flex the pomegranate to release the seeds, sprinkle over the salad, then chill until ready to serve.

For orange & fig refresher, make the syrup as above. Omit the grapefruit and increase the number of oranges to 6. Cut 4 fresh figs into wedges, peel, and add to the oranges. Add the sugar syrup and sprinkle with some fresh mint leaves. Serve chilled. Calories per serving 278

roasted pears with oriental spices

Calories per serving **279**
Serves **4**
Preparation time **20 minutes**
Cooking time **25 minutes**

4 **pears**
½ cup **dry** or **sweet sherry**
½ cup **water**
6–8 pieces **star anise**
1 **cinnamon stick**, broken
   into pieces
8 **cloves**
8 **cardamom pods**, crushed
3½ tablespoons **unsalted**
   butter
¼ cup firmly packed **light**
   brown sugar
1 **orange**

Leave the peel on the pears and cut them in half, down through the stems to the base. Scoop out the core, then put in a roasting pan with the cut sides up. Spoon the sherry into the core cavity of each pear and the measured water into the base of the pan. Sprinkle the spices over the pears, including the cardamom pods and their black seeds. Dot with the butter, then sprinkle with the sugar.

Remove the zest from the orange and sprinkle into the pan. Cut the orange into wedges and squeeze the juice over the pears. Add the wedges to the base of the roasting pan.

Cook in a preheated oven, at 350°F, for 25 minutes, until tender and just beginning to brown, spooning the pan juices over the pears halfway through cooking and again at the end.

Spoon into shallow dishes, drizzle with the pan juices, and serve with reduced-fat sour cream or Greek yogurt.

For roasted apples with peppercorns, core and halve 4 dessert apples, then place, cut side up, in a roasting pan. Spoon ¾ cup hard cider over the apples and into the roasting pan. Sprinkle with 1 teaspoon coarsely crushed multicolored peppercorns and 1 broken cinnamon stick. Dot with butter and sprinkle with sugar as above. Remove the zest from 1 lemon and reserve for decoration, then cut the lemon into wedges, squeeze the juice over the apples, and add the wedges to the base of the pan. Bake as above. **Calories per serving 251**

blood orange sorbet

Calories per serving **282**

Serves **4**

Preparation time **25 minutes**, plus chilling and freezing

Cooking time about **20 minutes**

1 ¼ cups **sugar**

1 cup **water**

pared peel of 2 **blood oranges**

1 ¼ cups **blood orange juice**

chilled **Campari**, to serve (optional)

orange peel, to decorate

Heat the sugar over low heat in a small saucepan with the measured water, stirring occasionally until completely dissolved.

Add the orange peel and increase the heat. Without stirring, boil the syrup for about 12 minutes, then set aside to cool completely.

When it is cold, strain the sugar syrup over the orange juice and stir together. Refrigerate for about 2 hours, until really cold.

Pour the chilled orange syrup into an ice-cream machine and churn for about 10 minutes. When the sorbet is almost frozen, scrape it into a plastic container and put it in the freezer compartment for an additional hour until completely frozen. Alternatively, pour the chilled orange syrup into a shallow metal container and put it in the freezer for 2 hours. Remove and whisk with a handheld electric mixer or balloon whisk, breaking up all the ice crystals. Return it to the freezer and repeat this process every hour or so until frozen.

Serve scoops of sorbet with a splash of chilled Campari, if desired, and decorate with thin strips of orange peel.

For papaya & lime sorbet, dissolve ⅔ cup sugar in ⅔ cup water. Boil for 5 minutes, then set aside to cool. Seed, peel, and dice the flesh of 1 ripe papaya. Process the papaya with the cooled sugar syrup. Stir in the grated zest and juice of 2 limes, chill, and proceed as above. **Calories per serving 181**

toffee & chocolate popcorn

Calories per serving **282**
Serves **12**
Preparation time **1 minute**
Cooking time **4 minutes**

½ cup **popping corn**
2¼ sticks **butter**
generous 2 cups firmly packed
  light brown sugar
2 tablespoons **unsweetened
  cocoa powder**

Microwave the popping corn in a large bowl with a lid on high (900 watts) for 4 minutes. Alternatively, cook in a saucepan with a lid on the stove, on medium heat, for a few minutes until popping.

Meanwhile, gently heat the butter, brown sugar, and cocoa powder in a saucepan until the sugar has dissolved and the butter has melted.

Stir the warm popcorn into the mixture and serve.

For toffee, marshmallow & nut popcorn, omit the brown sugar and cocoa. Microwave the popping corn as above, then gently heat 5 oz chewy toffees, 1 stick plus 1 tablespoon butter, 1¼ cups marshmallows, and 2 oz semisweet chocolate in a pan until melted. Serve as above. **Calories per serving 341**

hot cross buns

Calories per serving **287**

Makes **12**

Preparation time **1 hour**, plus standing and rising

Cooking time **20 minutes**

2 tablespoons **active dry yeast**

1 teaspoon **sugar**

²/₃ cup **milk**, warmed

4 tablespoons warm **water**

3²/₃ cups **bread flour**

1 teaspoon **salt**

½ teaspoon **ground pumpkin pie spice**

½ teaspoon **ground cinnamon**

½ teaspoon grated **nutmeg**

¼ cup **superfine sugar**

3½ tablespoons **butter**, melted and cooled

1 **egg**, beaten

¾ cup **currants**

¼ cup **chopped candied peel**

3 oz store-bought **shortcrust pastry**

For the glaze

3 tablespoons **superfine sugar**

4 tablespoons **milk** and **water**

Combine the yeast and sugar with the warmed milk and water. Stir into a scant cup of the flour. Leave in a warm place for about 20 minutes. Sift the remaining flour into a bowl. Add the salt, spices, and superfine sugar.

Add the butter and egg to the yeast mixture. Stir this into the flour and mix well. Add the dried fruit and mix to a fairly soft dough. Add a little water if necessary.

Turn out the dough onto a lightly floured surface and knead well. Place in an oiled plastic bag and let rise for 1–1½ hours at room temperature, until doubled in size. Turn out onto a floured surface and knead with your knuckles to knock out the air bubbles.

Divide the dough and shape into 12 round buns. Flatten each slightly, then space well apart on floured baking sheets. Cover and put in a warm place to rise for 20–30 minutes, until doubled in size. Meanwhile, thinly roll out the pastry and cut it into 24 thin strips about 3½ inches long.

Dampen the strips and lay 2, damp side down, in a cross over each bun. Bake in a preheated oven, at 375°F, for 20 minutes or until golden brown and firm.

Make the glaze. Dissolve the sugar in the milk and water mixture over low heat. Brush the cooked buns twice with the glaze. Serve hot, split, and buttered.

For gingered fruit buns, use ¾ cup luxury dried fruit instead of the currants, and 2 tablespoons chopped candied ginger in place of the candied peel. Omit the pastry crosses and glaze as above. **Calories per serving 285**

blueberry bakewell

Calories per serving **289**
Cuts into **18**
Preparation time **20 minutes**
Cooking time **1 hour**

11½ oz store-bought **sweet shortcrust pastry**
6 tablespoons **blueberry preserve** (see below for homemade)
1 stick plus 1 tablespoon **slightly salted butter**, softened
⅔ cup **superfine sugar**
2 **eggs**
1 cup **all-purpose flour**
1½ teaspoons **baking powder**
1 teaspoon **almond extract**
1 cup **ground almonds**
¼ cup **sliced almonds**
¾ cup **confectioners' sugar**, sifted

Roll out the pastry on a lightly floured surface and use to line a greased 11 x 7 inch shallow baking pan. Line the pastry shell with parchment paper and pie weights (or dried beans reserved for the purpose). Bake in a preheated oven, at 400°F, for 15 minutes. Remove the paper and weights and bake for another 5 minutes. Reduce the oven temperature to 350°F.

Spread the base of the pastry with the preserves. Beat together the butter, superfine sugar, eggs, flour, baking powder, and almond extract in a bowl until smooth and creamy. Beat in the ground almonds. Spoon the mixture over the preserves and spread gently in an even layer.

Sprinkle with the sliced almonds and bake in the oven for about 40 minutes, until risen and just firm to the touch. Let cool in the pan.

Beat the confectioners' sugar with a dash of water in a bowl to give the consistency of thin cream. Spread in a thin layer over the cake. Let set, then cut into squares or bars.

For homemade blueberry preserves, put 1 lb fresh blueberries, 4 tablespoons lemon juice, and 2 tablespoons water in a large saucepan and cook gently for about 8–10 minutes, until the berries are soft. Stir in 2¼ cups preserving or granulated sugar and heat gently until the sugar dissolves. Bring to a boil and boil for 10–15 minutes, until setting point is reached. Ladle into sterilized jars, cover, and label.
Calories per serving 141

mango & passion fruit trifle

Calories per serving **292**

Serves **4**

Preparation time **10 minutes**, plus chilling

4 **ladyfingers**

⅔ cup **full-fat Greek yogurt**

¾ cup **reduced-fat sour cream**

4 **passion fruit**

1 **mango**, peeled, pitted, and diced

Break each ladyfinger into 4 pieces and arrange them in 4 tumblers.

Mix together the yogurt and reduced-fat sour cream. Remove the seedy pulp from the passion fruit and set aside.

Spoon a little passion fruit pulp over the ladyfingers and add about half the mango pieces.

Pour about half the sour cream mix over the fruit and top with the remaining mango.

Top with the remaining sour cream mix and arrange the rest of the passion fruit on top. Refrigerate for up to 1 hour or serve immediately.

For pineapple & strawberry trifle, replace the mango with 2 cups peeled, diced pineapple and replace the passion fruit with ½ cup halved strawberries. You can also use any of the wide range of frozen fruit available, but make sure the fruit is fully thawed first. Continue as above. **Calories per serving 298**

chocolate sorbet

Calories per serving **295**
Serves **6–8**
Makes about **1 quart**
Preparation time **15 minutes**,
  plus chilling and freezing
Cooking time **10 minutes**

2½ cups **water**
⅔ cup firmly packed **dark
  brown sugar**
1 cup **granulated sugar**
½ cup **unsweetened cocoa
  powder**
1 oz **bittersweet chocolate**
  with 70% cocoa solids,
  finely chopped
2½ teaspoons **vanilla extract**
1 teaspoon **instant espresso
  coffee powder**

Put the measured water, sugars, and cocoa powder in a saucepan and mix together. Heat gently, stirring until the sugar has dissolved. Increase the heat to bring the mixture to a boil, then reduce to a simmer for 8 minutes.

Remove the pan from the heat and stir in the chocolate, vanilla extract, and espresso powder until thoroughly dissolved. Pour into a bowl and cool over ice or leave to cool and chill.

Freeze in an ice-cream machine according to the manufacturer's instructions. Serve immediately or transfer to a chilled plastic freezerproof container and store in the freezer for up to 1 month. If you are using the sorbet straight from the freezer, transfer to the refrigerator 20 minutes before serving to soften slightly.

For rum & chocolate-chip sorbet, replace the vanilla extract with 3 tablespoons dark rum. Stir 3 oz chopped bittersweet chocolate into the ice-cream mixture before churning. **Calories per serving 397**

moroccan baked figs with yogurt

Calories per serving **298**
Serves **4**
Preparation time **10 minutes**
Cooking time **10 minutes**

8 **fresh figs**, rinsed in cold
    water
about 3 teaspoons **rose water**
¼ cup **honey**
3½ tablespoons **unsalted
    butter**
1 cup **Greek yogurt**
a little **Turkish delight**,
    coarsely chopped

Cut a cross in the top of each fig and open out the cut
to halfway through the fruit. Arrange the figs in a small
roasting pan or shallow ovenproof dish. Add a few drops
of rose water to each fig, then drizzle with 3 tablespoons
of the honey and dot with the butter.

Bake in a preheated oven, at 375°F, for 8–10 minutes,
until the figs are hot but still firm. Meanwhile, mix the
yogurt with the remaining honey and gradually mix in
a little of the remaining rose water to taste.

Transfer the figs to shallow serving dishes and serve
with spoonfuls of yogurt sprinkled with Turkish delight.

For orange & pistachio baked apricots, arrange
12 fresh apricots, halved, in a roasting pan. Add a few
drops of orange flower water to each apricot half, then
drizzle with 3 tablespoons honey and sprinkle with
¼ cup halved pistachio nuts. Dot with 3½ tablespoons
butter and bake as above. Serve with 1 cup Greek
yogurt flavored with 1 tablespoon honey and orange
flower water to taste. **Calories per serving 310**

recipes under 400 calories

chai tea bread

Calories per serving **302**

Cuts into **10**

Preparation time **15 minutes**, plus standing

Cooking time **1 ¼ hours**

5 **chai tea bags**

1 ¼ cups **boiling water**

2 cups **all-purpose flour**

3 teaspoons **baking powder**

1 ½ cups firmly packed **light brown sugar**

1 ¾ cups **mixed dried fruit**

⅓ cup **Brazil nuts**, chopped

3 ½ tablespoons **butter**

1 **egg**, beaten

Stir the tea bags into the measured water in a pitcher and let stand for 10 minutes.

Mix together the flour, baking powder, sugar, dried fruit, and nuts in a bowl. Remove the tea bags from the water, pressing them against the side of the pitcher to squeeze out all the water. Thinly slice the butter into the water and stir until melted. Let cool slightly. Add to the dry ingredients with the egg and mix together well.

Spoon the mixture into a greased and lined 2 lb or 5 ¼ cup loaf pan and spread the mixture into the corners. Bake in a preheated oven, at 325°F, for 1 ¼ hours or until risen, firm, and a toothpick inserted into the center comes out clean. Loosen the cake at the ends and transfer to a wire rack. Peel off the lining paper and let cool. Spread the top with chai cream frosting, if desired (see below).

For chai cream frosting, to spread over the cake, put 3 tablespoons milk and 3 chai tea bags in a saucepan and bring to a boil. Remove from the heat and leave the tea bags to infuse in the milk until cold. Discard the tea bags, squeezing them to extract the liquid. Beat together ¾ cup cream cheese and 2 tablespoons very soft unsalted butter in a bowl until smooth. Beat in the flavored milk and ¾ cup sifted confectioners' sugar. **Calories per serving 113**

black forest brownies

Calories per serving **317**
Cuts into **12**
Preparation time **25 minutes**
Cooking time **25–30 minutes**

5 oz **semisweet chocolate**, chopped
1 stick plus 1 tablespoon **slightly salted butter**
2 **eggs**
¾ cup firmly packed **dark brown sugar**
1 teaspoon **vanilla extract**
⅓ cup **all-purpose flour**
⅓ teaspoon **baking powder**
1 cup **black** or **red cherries**, pitted and halved, plus extra to serve

To serve
⅔ cup **heavy cream**
chocolate shavings

Melt 2 oz of the chocolate and the butter in a heatproof bowl set over a saucepan of gently simmering water (don't let the base of the bowl touch the water).

Beat the eggs, sugar, and vanilla in a separate bowl until light and foamy. Stir in the melted chocolate mixture. Tip in the flour, cherries, and remaining chocolate and mix together until just combined.

Spoon the mixture into a greased and lined 7 inch square cake pan or shallow baking pan and level the surface. Bake in a preheated oven, at 350°F, for 20–25 minutes or until just firm to the touch. Let cool in the pan, then transfer to a board and peel off the lining paper.

Whip the cream in a bowl until peaking, then spread over the cake. Sprinkle with chocolate shavings and cut into small squares. Serve with extra cherries and rich chocolate sauce, if desired (see below).

For rich chocolate sauce, to serve as an accompaniment, heat ⅔ cup sugar and 5 tablespoons water in a small saucepan until the sugar dissolves. Bring to a boil and boil for 3 minutes. Remove from the heat and cool for 5 minutes. Add 5 oz chopped semisweet chocolate and 2 tablespoons diced unsalted butter and let stand, stirring frequently, until melted and smooth. If pieces of chocolate remain, reheat the sauce very gently.
Calories per serving 128

warm chocolate pots

Calories per serving **327**
Serves **6**
Preparation time **1 minute**
Cooking time **4 minutes**

10 oz **semisweet chocolate**
2 cups **fat-free fromage frais**
  or **plain yogurt**
1 teaspoon **vanilla extract**

Melt the chocolate in a bowl over a pan of simmering water, then remove from the heat.

Add the fromage frais and vanilla extract and quickly stir together.

Divide the chocolate fromage frais among 6 little pots or glasses and serve immediately.

For warm cappuccino pots, melt the semisweet chocolate with 2 tablespoons very strong espresso coffee and add the fat-free fromage frais or yogurt. Divide among 6 espresso cups, finishing each with 1 teaspoon regular fromage frais or yogurt and a dusting of unsweetened cocoa powder.
Calories per serving 339

blueberry meringue roulade

Calories per serving **336**

Cuts into **8**

Preparation time **30 minutes**, plus cooling

Cooking time **15 minutes**

4 **egg whites**

1¼ cups **superfine sugar**, plus extra for sprinkling

1 teaspoon **white wine vinegar**

1 teaspoon **cornstarch**

For the filling

grated zest of 1 **lime**

1¼ cups **heavy cream**, whipped

1¼ cups **blueberries**

3 **passion fruit**, halved

Whisk the egg whites in a large clean bowl until stiff. Gradually whisk in the sugar, a teaspoonful at time, until it has all been added. Whisk for a few minutes more until the meringue mixture is thick and glossy.

Combine the vinegar and cornstarch, then whisk into the meringue mixture. Spoon into a 13 x 9 inch jelly-roll pan lined with nonstick parchment paper that stands a little above the top of the pan sides, then spread the surface level. Bake in a preheated oven, at 375°F, for 10 minutes, until pale brown and well risen, then reduce the heat to 325°F, for 5 minutes, until just firm to the touch and the top is slightly cracked.

Meanwhile, cover a clean dish towel with nonstick parchment paper and sprinkle with a little sugar. Turn out the meringue onto the paper. Let cool for 1–2 hours. Carefully peel off the lining paper.

Fold the lime zest into the whipped cream. Spread over the meringue, then sprinkle with the blueberries and passion fruit seeds. Starting with a short side and using the paper to help, roll up the meringue to form a log. Serve the same day.

For minted strawberry roulade, spread the meringue with whipped cream folded with a small bunch of mint, freshly chopped, and 1 cup strawberries, coarsely chopped. Make the roulade as above and decorate with halved baby strawberries and mint leaves dusted with sifted confectioners' sugar. **Calories per serving 335**

mango & vanilla muffin slice

Calories per serving **336**
Cuts into **8**
Preparation time **20 minutes**
Cooking time **1 hour**

1 small **ripe mango**
1¾ cups **all-purpose flour**
2 teaspoons **baking powder**
¾ cup **unrefined superfine sugar**
½ cup **rolled oats**
1 **egg**, beaten
¾ cup **milk**
1 teaspoon **vanilla bean paste** or extract
7 tablespoons **slightly salted butter**, melted
vanilla sugar, for sprinkling

Halve the mango each side of the flat central pit. Cut away the pit, then peel and dice the flesh into ¼ inch pieces.

Sift the flour and baking powder into a bowl, then stir in the superfine sugar and oats. Beat together the egg, milk, vanilla, and melted butter in a pitcher. Add to the dry ingredients with half the mango and stir together using a large metal spoon until just combined.

Spoon the batter into a greased and lined 2 lb or 5¼ cup loaf pan. Sprinkle with the remaining mango pieces and bake in a preheated oven, at 350°F, for about 1 hour or until well risen, firm to the touch, and a toothpick inserted into the center comes out clean.

Let cool in the pan for 5 minutes, then loosen at the ends and transfer to a wire rack to cool. Peel off the lining paper and serve warm or cold, sprinkled with vanilla sugar.

For blueberry breakfast slice, put ½ cup dried blueberries, chopped, and 3 tablespoons apple or orange juice in a small saucepan and heat until the juice bubbles, then remove from the heat. Let cool until the juice is absorbed. Make the cake as above, omitting the mango and vanilla and adding 1 teaspoon ground cinnamon to the dry ingredients. Stir the blueberries and juice into the cake batter. Spoon into the pan and sprinkle with 2 tablespoons rolled oats. Bake as above. **Calories per serving 385**

simple iced buns

Calories per serving **345**
Makes **10**
Preparation time **25 minutes**,
  plus rising
Cooking time **12–15 minutes**

3²/₃ cups **bread flour**
¼ cup **superfine sugar**
1 tablespoon **active dry yeast**
2 tablespoons **slightly salted
  butter**, melted
1¼ cups **hand-hot milk**, plus
  extra if required
2 teaspoons **vanilla extract**

For the icing
3¹/₃ cups **fondant sugar**
pink food coloring

Mix together the flour, sugar, and yeast in a bowl.
Add the butter, milk, and vanilla and mix to a fairly soft
dough, adding a dash more milk or hot water if the
dough feels dry. Knead the dough for 10 minutes on a
floured surface, until smooth and elastic. Put in a lightly
oiled bowl, cover with plastic wrap, and let rise in a warm
place for about 1 hour or until doubled in size.

Punch the dough to deflate it, then divide into 10
even-size pieces on a floured surface and shape each
into a sausage shape. Place, well spaced apart, on a
large greased baking sheet. Cover loosely with greased
plastic wrap and let rise for 30 minutes.

Bake in a preheated oven, at 400°F, for 12–15 minutes,
until risen and pale golden (placing a roasting pan filled
with ¾ inch hot water on the lower shelf to prevent a
firm crust forming). Transfer to a wire rack to cool.

Make the icing. Sift the fondant sugar into a bowl and
gradually beat in a little water, a teaspoonful at a time,
to make a smooth, spreadable icing. Spread half over
5 of the buns. Add a dash of pink food coloring to the
remaining icing and spread over the rest of the buns.
Best eaten freshly baked.

For sticky currant buns, make the dough as above,
adding ½ teaspoon ground cinnamon and 1 cup
mixed dried fruit. Let rise as above. Shape into 10 balls
and flatten slightly on the baking sheet. Brush with a
little milk and bake as above. Heat 2 tablespoons light
corn syrup in a saucepan and brush over the cooled
buns. **Calories per serving 286**

passion fruit yogurt fool

Calories per serving **347**
Serves **4**
Preparation time **8 minutes**

6 **passion fruit**, halved, flesh
  and seeds removed
1¼ cups **fat-free Greek
  yogurt**
1 tablespoon **honey**
¾ cup **whipping cream**,
  whipped to soft peaks
4 pieces of **shortbread**, to
  serve

Stir the passion fruit flesh and seeds into the yogurt
with the honey.

Fold the cream into the yogurt. Spoon into tall glasses
and serve with the shortbread.

For mango & lime yogurt fool, omit the passion
fruit, instead pureeing 1 large ripe peeled and pitted
mango with the zest of 1 lime and confectioners' sugar
to taste. Mix into the yogurt and fold in the cream.
Omit the honey. **Calories per serving 358**

spiced bananas

Calories per serving **348**
Serves **8**
Preparation time **10 minutes**
Cooking time **10 minutes**

8 **bananas**, peeled
2 tablespoons **lemon juice**
8 tablespoons firmly packed
  light brown sugar
3½ tablespoons **butter**,
  softened
1 teaspoon **cinnamon**

Rum mascarpone cream
1 cup **mascarpone cheese**
2 tablespoons **rum**
1–2 tablespoons **granulated
  sugar**

Put each banana on a double piece of foil. Drizzle over the lemon juice and sprinkle 1 tablespoon of the brown sugar on each banana.

Beat together the butter and cinnamon in a bowl until creamy, then spoon over the bananas. Wrap each banana tightly in the foil and cook over a barbecue or under a preheated medium broiler for 10 minutes.

Meanwhile, make the rum mascarpone cream. Mix together the mascarpone, rum, and sugar in a bowl.

Unwrap the bananas and slice thickly. Serve immediately with the rum mascarpone cream.

For BBQ pineapple with rum butter glaze, cut off the top and base of 1 large fresh pineapple and slice off the skin, then cut into quarters and remove the core from each quarter. Slice the quarters across into 1 inch thick triangular slices. Sprinkle both sides with a little sugar and cook over a barbecue for 5–6 minutes or until lightly caramelized. Meanwhile, melt 5 tablespoons butter in a small pan, then add ⅓ cup Demerara sugar and the juice of ½ lime. Scrape out the seeds of 1 vanilla bean and add to the pan with 2 tablespoons dark rum. Stir until the mixture has melted and bubbled to form a smooth glaze. Place the pineapple slices on a plate, spoon over the rum butter, and serve immediately with 1 scoop ice cream per slice. **Calories per serving 248**

pears with minted mascarpone

Calories per serving **358**
Serves **4**
Preparation time **10 minutes**
Cooking time **5 minutes**

2 tablespoons **unsalted butter**
2 tablespoons **honey**
4 ripe **dessert pears**, such as Red William, cored and quartered lengthwise
lemon juice, for sprinkling

Minted mascarpone
1 tablespoon **fresh mint**, finely chopped
1 tablespoon **sugar**
¾ cup **mascarpone cheese**

To decorate
fresh mint sprigs
confectioners' sugar, sifted
ground cinnamon

Melt the butter in a small saucepan. Remove the pan from the heat and stir in the honey.

Sprinkle the pear slices with a little lemon juice as soon as they are cut to prevent them from discoloring. Line a baking sheet with foil and lay the pear slices on it. Brush the pears with the butter and honey mixture and cook under a preheated broiler on its highest setting for 5 minutes.

Meanwhile, make the minted mascarpone. Lightly beat the mint and sugar into the mascarpone in a bowl.

Arrange the pear slices on 4 plates and top each with a spoonful of the minted mascarpone. Decorate with mint sprigs, then lightly dust with confectioners' sugar and cinnamon and serve immediately.

For pear & jelly tarts, lay out 7 oz ready-rolled puff pastry, thawed if frozen, on a floured surface and cut out 4 circles using a 7 inch plate as a template. Transfer the circles to 2 greased baking sheets. Peel, core, and finely slice the pears and place in a bowl. Toss with just enough sugar to coat the fruit and 2 tablespoons freshly squeezed orange juice. Place 1 tablespoon any flavored jelly in the middle of each pastry circle, fan out the fruit slices on top and fold in the sides of the pastry to hold it all together. Bake in a preheated oven, at 425°F, for 10–12 minutes, until the fruit has softened and the pastry is crisp and golden. Serve with 1 scoop vanilla ice cream per tart. **Calories per serving 401**

watermelon & choc-chip sorbet

Calories per serving **358**
Serves **8**
Preparation time **20 minutes**,
  plus chilling and freezing
Cooking time **5 minutes**

1½ lb **peeled watermelon**,
  seeded and cubed
1½ cups **superfine sugar**
½ cup **lemon juice**
pink food coloring (optional)
1 **egg white**
⅔ cup **chocolate chips**

Puree the watermelon in a food processor or blender. Add the sugar and process for 30 seconds.

Pour into a saucepan and bring slowly to a boil, stirring until the sugar has dissolved, then simmer for 1 minute. Remove from the heat, add the lemon juice, then let cool, adding a few drops of pink food coloring, if desired. Chill for at least 1 hour or overnight.

Use an ice-cream machine for the best results. Half-freeze the mixture according to the manufacturer's instructions, then lightly whisk the egg white and add with the motor still running. Stir in the chocolate chips, then transfer to a plastic freezerproof container and freeze until firm.

Alternatively, freeze the mixture in a shallow freezer container until frozen around the edges, then mash well with a fork. Whisk the egg white until stiff in a bowl. Drop spoonfuls of the sorbet into the egg white while whisking constantly with a handheld electric mixer until the mixture is thick and foamy. Return to the freezer to firm up, then stir in the chocolate chips when almost frozen. Freeze until firm.

Transfer the sorbet to the refrigerator for 20 minutes before serving to soften. Serve with dessert cookies.

For watermelon & orange sorbet, omit the chocolate chips. Reduce the quantity of watermelon to 1 lb and process to a puree. Heat the sugar in a pan with 1 cup freshly squeezed orange juice, stirring until dissolved. Once cooled combine the watermelon, sweetened orange juice, and lemon juice. Freeze as above.
Calories per serving 246

mixed berry chocolate roulade

Calories per serving **364**

Serves **4**

Preparation time **20 minutes**, plus cooling

Cooking time **15 minutes**

3 **large eggs**

½ cup **superfine sugar**

½ teaspoon **chocolate extract**

⅓ cup **all-purpose flour**

¼ cup **unsweetened cocoa powder**, plus extra to dust

⅔ cup **reduced-fat sour cream**

⅔ cup **fat-free Greek yogurt**

3 tablespoons **confectioners' sugar**

1 tablespoon **chocolate sauce**

1 cup **mixed berries**, chopped, plus extra to decorate

Grease and line a 12 x 8 inch jelly-roll pan. Whisk together the eggs and sugar until the beater leaves a trail over the surface. Add the chocolate extract, sift in the flour and cocoa, and fold in carefully.

Pour the batter into the prepared pan. Bake in a preheated oven, at 400°F, for 15 minutes. Place a clean dish towel on the work surface and put a piece of nonstick parchment paper on top. When the sponge is cooked, turn it out onto the parchment paper, roll it up carefully and let cool.

Mix together the reduced-fat sour cream, yogurt, confectioners' sugar, and chocolate sauce.

Unroll the roulade and spread the sour cream mix over it. Spoon the berries over the sour cream and roll up the roulade again. Dust with cocoa and serve immediately, decorated with extra berries.

For strawberry & vanilla roulade, omit the cocoa, increase the all-purpose flour to ⅔ cup and use ½ teaspoon vanilla extract instead of the chocolate extract. Use 1 cup strawberries to fill the roulade and serve decorated with extra sliced strawberries, if desired. **Calories per serving 381**

peach & blueberry crunch

Calories per serving **371**
Serves **4**
Preparation time **8 minutes**
Cooking time **8–10 minutes**

¼ cup **ground hazelnuts**
¼ cup **ground almonds**
2 tablespoons **superfine sugar**
½ cup **bread crumbs**
13½ oz can **peaches** in natural juice
1 cup **blueberries**
⅔ cup **heavy cream**
seeds from 1 **vanilla bean**
1 tablespoon **confectioners' sugar**, sifted

Gently cook the ground nuts in a large skillet with the sugar and bread crumbs, stirring constantly until golden. Remove from the heat and let cool.

Put the peaches in a food processor or blender and blend with enough of the peach juice to make a thick, smooth puree.

Set aside some of the blueberries to decorate and fold the remaining blueberries gently into the puree. Spoon into 4 glasses or individual serving dishes.

Whip the cream with the vanilla seeds and confectioners' sugar until thick but not stiff and spoon evenly over the peach puree. When the crunchy topping is cool, sprinkle it over the blueberry mixture, top with the remaining blueberries, and serve.

For apple & blackberry cracker crunch, peel 1 lb cooking apples and cook with 2–3 tablespoons sugar and 2 tablespoons water. Fold 1 cup blackberries into the apple puree and continue as above, but instead of bread crumbs, use crushed graham crackers. Use the same amount and toast in the same way, but reduce the sugar to 1 tablespoon. **Calories per serving 393**

date & banana ripple slice

Calories per serving **373**

Cuts into **10**

Preparation time **20 minutes**,
  plus cooling

Cooking time **1 hour 25
  minutes**

1½ cups **pitted dates**, roughly
  chopped

finely grated zest and juice of
  1 lemon

scant ½ cup **water**

2 small very **ripe bananas**

1 stick plus 3 tablespoons
  slightly salted butter,
  softened

¾ cup **superfine sugar**

2 **eggs**

scant ½ cup **milk**

2¼ cups **all-purpose flour**

3¼ teaspoons **baking powder**

Put 1¼ cups of the dates in a small saucepan with
the lemon zest and juice and measured water. Bring
to a boil, then reduce the heat and simmer gently for
5 minutes, until the dates are soft and pulpy. Mash
the mixture with a fork until fairly smooth. Let cool.

Mash the bananas to a puree in a bowl, then add the
butter, sugar, eggs, milk, flour, and baking powder and
beat together until smooth.

Spoon a third of the batter into a greased and lined
2½ lb or 6 cup loaf pan and level the surface. Spoon
over half the date puree and spread evenly. Add
half the remaining cake batter and spread with the
remaining puree. Add the remaining cake batter and
level the surface.

Sprinkle with the remaining dates and bake in a
preheated oven, at 325°F, for about 1 hour 20 minutes
or until risen and a toothpick inserted into the center
comes out clean. Let cool in the pan for 15 minutes,
then loosen at the ends and transfer to a wire rack. Peel
off the lining paper and let the cake cool completely.

For honeyed banana cake, make the cake as above,
omitting all the dates. For the honey buttercream,
beat together 1 stick plus 3 tablespoons softened
unsalted butter, 6 tablespoons sifted confectioners'
sugar, and 6 tablespoons honey in a bowl until smooth
and creamy. Spread over the top of the cooled cake.
Calories per serving 447

chocolate cupcakes

Calories per serving **374**
Makes **12**
Preparation time **10 minutes**,
  plus cooling
Cooking time **18–20 minutes**
Decoration time **20 minutes**

1 stick plus 3 tablespoons
  butter or **margarine**
¾ cup **superfine sugar**
1⅓ cups **all-purpose flour**
1⅓ teaspoons **baking
  powder**
3 **eggs**
1 teaspoon **vanilla extract**

To decorate
4 oz **white chocolate**,
  chopped
4 oz **milk chocolate**, chopped
4 oz **semisweet chocolate**,
  chopped
3 tablespoons **butter**
unsweetened cocoa powder,
  for dusting

Beat the butter or margarine, sugar, flour, eggs, and vanilla extract in a mixing bowl until light and creamy.

Line a 12-cup muffin pan with paper liners. Divide the mixture evenly among the liners and bake in a preheated oven, at 350°F, for 18–20 minutes, until risen and just firm to the touch. Transfer to a wire rack to cool.

Melt the white, milk, and semisweet chocolate in 3 separate bowls, each with one-third of the butter added, over pans of simmering water. Spread the melted white chocolate over 4 of the cakes and dust with a little cocoa powder.

Put 2 tablespoons each of the melted milk chocolate and semisweet chocolate in separate pastry bags fitted with decorator tips. Spread the milk chocolate over 4 more of the cakes and pipe dots of semisweet chocolate over the milk chocolate. Spread the semisweet chocolate over the 4 remaining cakes and scribble with lines of piped milk chocolate.

For triple chocolate cupcakes, substitute 2 tablespoons unsweetened cocoa powder for 2 tablespoons of the flour and add 2 oz chopped white chocolate. Prepare the mixture and bake as above. Decorate the cooled cakes with white chocolate fudge icing made by melting 8 oz white chocolate with ½ cup light cream and 5 tablespoons butter. Cool, then beat until thick and fluffy before piping a large swirl on each cake. **Calories per serving 412**

ricotta & maple syrup cheesecake

Calories per serving **375**

Serves **8**

Preparation time **20 minutes**, plus chilling

3 **gelatin leaves**

1½ cups crushed **graham crackers**

3½ tablespoons **reduced-fat sunflower spread**, melted

¾ cup **cottage cheese**

¾ cup **ricotta cheese**

2 **egg whites**

¼ cup **confectioners' sugar**, sifted

1½ tablespoons **lemon juice**

¼ cup **maple syrup**

To decorate

2 **oranges**, peeled and sliced

sprigs of **red currants**

Line an 8 inch springform cake pan with nonstick parchment paper. Soften the gelatin in cold water.

Mix together the cracker crumbs and melted sunflower spread and press into the prepared pan. Refrigerate.

Sieve together the cottage cheese and ricotta. Beat the egg whites until stiffly peaking, then beat in the confectioners' sugar until glossy.

Put the lemon juice and 3 tablespoons water in a saucepan over low heat and stir in the gelatin until dissolved. Add to the ricotta mix with the maple syrup, then fold in the egg whites. Pour the mixture over the crumb crust and refrigerate until set.

Decorate with the sliced oranges and sprigs of red currants before serving.

For raspberry & ricotta cheesecake with chocolate sauce, stir 2 cups raspberries into the ricotta mix, then make the cheesecake as above. To serve, melt 4 oz semisweet chocolate with ¼ cup syrup and drizzle over the cheesecake. **Calories per serving 460**

instant apple crumbles

Calories per serving **379**
Serves **4**
Preparation time **7 minutes**
Cooking time **13 minutes**

2 lb **cooking apples**, peeled,
  cored, and thickly sliced
2 tablespoons **butter**
2 tablespoons **sugar**
1 tablespoon **lemon juice**
2 tablespoons **water**

Crumble
3½ tablespoons **butter**
1½ cups fresh **whole-wheat
  bread crumbs**
¼ cup **pumpkin seeds**
2 tablespoons packed **brown
  sugar**

Place the apples in a saucepan with the butter, sugar,
lemon juice, and measured water. Cover and simmer
for 8–10 minutes, until softened.

Melt the butter for the crumble in a skillet, add the
bread crumbs, and stir-fry until lightly golden, then add
the pumpkin seeds and stir-fry for another 1 minute.
Remove from the heat and stir in the brown sugar.

Spoon the apple mixture into bowls and sprinkle with
the crumble.

For instant pear & chocolate crumble, cook
2 lb pears in the butter, sugar, and water as above,
adding ½ teaspoon ground ginger to the butter.
Prepare the crumble as above, replacing the pumpkin
seeds with 2 oz coarsely chopped semisweet chocolate.
Cook as above. Calories per serving 424

poached fruit with ginger cookies

Calories per serving **391**
Serves **6**
Preparation time **15 minutes**
Cooking time **20 minutes**

1¼ cups **superfine sugar**
2½ quarts **water**
1 **vanilla bean**, plus extra for
  decorating if desired
4 **peaches**
4 **nectarines**
10 **apricots**

To serve
mascarpone cheese
3 **ginger cookies**, crushed

Put the sugar, measured water, and vanilla bean in a large, heavy saucepan and heat gently, stirring, until the sugar has dissolved. Bring to a low simmer, add the fruit, and cover with a circle of wax or parchment paper to hold the fruit in the syrup. Simmer for 2 minutes, then turn off the heat and let cool.

Remove the fruit from the liquid with a slotted spoon, reserving the poaching liquid. Peel the skins from the fruit, then cut them in half and remove the pits.

Put 1 cup of the poaching liquid in a small, heavy saucepan and heat to reduce it for 6–8 minutes, until it has a syrupy consistency. Put the fruit in a large bowl, pour over the syrup, and toss gently. Arrange the fruit on serving plates, add 1 rounded tablespoon mascarpone to each one and sprinkle with crushed ginger cookies. Decorate with a vanilla bean, if desired.

For poached stone fruit with raspberry coulis, put 1¼ cups frozen raspberries and 3 tablespoons sugar in a heavy saucepan. Slowly bring up to a boil, stirring, to dissolve the sugar. Simmer for 2–3 minutes, until the coulis has a syrupy consistency. Remove from the heat and strain through a fine sieve. Poach the stone fruit as above and serve with the raspberry coulis and a drizzle of custard. **Calories per serving 322**

granola squares

Calories per serving **399**
Makes **12**
Preparation time **15 minutes**,
   plus chilling
Cooking time **20 minutes**

1 ½ sticks **butter**, plus extra for
   greasing
⅔ cup **honey**
2 tablespoons **maple syrup**
1 teaspoon **ground cinnamon**
¾ cup ready-to-eat **dried
   apricots**, coarsely chopped
¾ cup ready-to-eat **dried
   papaya** or **mango**, coarsely
   chopped
¾ cup **raisins**
¼ cup **pumpkin seeds**
2 tablespoons **sesame seeds**
3 tablespoons **sunflower
   seeds**
¾ cup **pecan nuts**, coarsely
   chopped
2¾ cups **rolled oats**

Grease an 11 x 7 inch deep jelly-roll pan with butter and line the bottom with nonstick parchment paper.

Place the butter, honey, and maple syrup in a medium saucepan and heat, stirring continually, until the butter has melted. Add the cinnamon, dried fruit, seeds, and nuts, stir the mixture, and heat for 1 minute. Remove from the heat and add the rolled oats, stirring until they are well coated in the syrup.

Transfer the mixture to the prepared pan and smooth down with the back of a spoon to compact into the pan and level. Bake in a preheated oven, at 350°F, for 15 minutes, until the top is just beginning to brown. Remove from the oven and let cool in the pan, then chill in the refrigerator for 30–60 minutes.

Turn out the chilled granola, upside down, on a chopping board, then carefully flip it back over to its correct side. Using a long, sharp knife (preferably longer than the granola itself), cut into 12 squares.

For fruity chocolate granola squares, leave out the pecans and seeds and replace with 3 oz coarsely chopped ready-to-eat dried apples. Once cooled, drizzle 2 oz melted white chocolate over the top. Allow to set in the refrigerator for 10 minutes before cutting into squares. **Calories per serving 360**

recipes
under 500
calories

lemon drizzle cake

Calories per serving **400**
Cuts into **8**
Preparation time **20 minutes**
Cooking time **22–28 minutes**

5 **eggs**
½ cup **superfine sugar**
pinch of **salt**
1 cup **all-purpose flour**
1 teaspoon **baking powder**
finely grated zest of 1 **lemon**
1 tablespoon **lemon juice**
7 tablespoons **butter**, melted
   and cooled

For the syrup
2½ cups **confectioners'**
   sugar, sifted
½ cup **lemon juice**
finely grated zest of 1 **lemon**
seeds scraped from 1 **vanilla**
   bean

Put the eggs, sugar, and salt in a large heatproof bowl set over a saucepan of barely simmering water and beat with a handheld electric mixer for 2–3 minutes or until it triples in volume and thickens to the consistency of lightly whipped cream. Remove from the heat. Sift in the flour and baking powder, add the lemon zest and juice and drizzle the butter down the side of the bowl. Fold in gently.

Pour the batter into a greased and lined 8½ inch square cake pan. Bake in a preheated oven, at 350°F, for 20–25 minutes or until risen, golden, and coming away from the sides of the pan.

Meanwhile, put all the syrup ingredients in a small saucepan and heat gently until the sugar dissolves. Increase the heat and boil rapidly for 4–5 minutes. Set aside to cool a little.

Let the cake cool in the pan for 5 minutes, then make holes over the surface with a toothpick. Drizzle over two-thirds of the warm syrup. Let the cake cool and absorb the syrup. Turn the cake out of the pan and peel off the lining paper. Cut into squares or slices and serve with 1 heaping teaspoon of reduced-fat sour cream and an extra drizzle of syrup.

For citrus drizzle cake with sorbet, make the cake as above, replacing the lemon zest and juice with the finely grated zest of 1 orange and 1 tablespoon orange juice. Serve topped with lemon sorbet. **Calories per serving 391**

tuile baskets & strawberry cream

Calories per serving **404**
Serves **6**
Preparation time **40 minutes**
Cooking time **15–18 minutes**

2 **egg whites**
½ cup **superfine sugar**
3½ tablespoons **unsalted butter**, melted
few drops **vanilla extract**
⅓ cup **all-purpose flour**

Strawberry cream
1 cup **heavy cream**
¼ cup **confectioners' sugar**, plus extra for dusting
2 tablespoons **chopped fresh mint**, plus extra leaves to decorate
1½ cups **strawberries**, halved or sliced, depending on size

Put the egg whites in a bowl and break up with a fork. Stir in the superfine sugar, then the butter and vanilla extract. Sift in the flour and mix until smooth.

Drop 1 heaping tablespoon of the mixture onto a baking sheet lined with nonstick parchment paper. Drop a second spoonful well apart from the first, then spread each into a thin circle about 5 inches in diameter. Bake in a preheated oven, at 375°F, for 5–6 minutes, until just beginning to brown around the edges.

Add 2 more spoonfuls to a second paper-lined baking sheet and spread thinly. Remove the baked tuiles from the oven and put the second tray in. Allow the cooked tuiles to firm up for 5–10 seconds, then carefully lift them off the paper one at a time and drape each over an orange. Pinch the edges into pleats and let harden for 2–3 minutes, then carefully ease off. Repeat until 6 tuiles have been made.

Whip the cream lightly, then fold in half the sugar, the mint and the strawberries, reserving 6 strawberry halves for decoration. Spoon into the tuiles, then top with the mint leaves and the strawberry halves. Dust with sifted confectioners' sugar.

For fruit salad baskets, make the tuiles as above and fill with 1 cup sliced strawberries, ¾ cup halved seedless ruby grapes, 2 kiwifruits, peeled, halved, and sliced, and 2 small ripe peaches. Top each one with 1 tablespoon Greek yogurt and 1 teaspoon honey.
Calories per serving 247

caramelized clementines with bay

Calories per serving **405**
Serves **4**
Preparation time **10 minutes**
Cooking time **12 minutes**

1¼ cups **sugar**
1 cup **cold water**
8 **clementines**
4 small **fresh bay leaves**
6 tablespoons **boiling water**
4 tablespoons **reduced-fat
    sour cream**, to serve

Put the sugar and measured cold water in a saucepan and heat gently, stirring very occasionally until the sugar has completely dissolved.

Meanwhile, peel the clementines and, leaving them whole, place in a heavy glass serving bowl or mixing bowl with the bay leaves.

Increase the heat once the sugar has dissolved and boil the syrup for 8–10 minutes, without stirring and keeping a close watch on it until it begins to change color, first becoming pale golden around the edges, then a rich golden color all over.

Take the pan off the heat, then add the measured boiling water, a tablespoon at a time, standing well back in case the syrup spits. Tilt the pan to mix but don't stir. Once the bubbles have subsided, pour the hot syrup over the clementines and bay leaves. Let cool, then serve the dessert with 1 tablespoon reduced-fat sour cream per person.

For caramelized clementines with whole spices, omit the bay leaves and add 2 whole star anise or the equivalent in pieces, 1 cinnamon stick, halved, and 3 cloves to the clementines. Make the syrup as above, then pour it over the spices and fruit. **Calories per serving 405**

layered nutty bars

Calories per serving **406**

Cuts into **10**

Preparation time **20 minutes**,
 plus chilling

Cooking time **5 minutes**

3½ tablespoons **butter**

1¼ cups **fat-free sweetened condensed milk**

7 oz **semisweet chocolate**, broken into pieces

4 oz **rich tea biscuits**

⅓ cup **hazelnuts**

1 cup **pistachio nuts**, shelled

Use a little of the butter to grease the bottom and sides of an 8 inch round springform cake pan. Put the rest of the butter in a saucepan with the condensed milk and chocolate. Heat gently for 3–4 minutes, stirring until melted, then remove from the heat.

Place the biscuits in a plastic bag and crush roughly into chunky pieces using a rolling pin. Toast the hazelnuts under a preheated hot broiler until lightly browned, then roughly chop with the pistachios.

Stir the biscuits into the chocolate mixture, then spoon half the mixture into the prepared pan and spread level. Reserve 2 tablespoons of the nuts for the top, then sprinkle the rest over the chocolate biscuit layer. Cover with the remaining chocolate mixture, level the surface with the back of the spoon and sprinkle with the reserved nuts.

Chill the nut mixture for 3–4 hours, until firm, then loosen the edges and remove the sides of the pan. Cut into 10 thin slices, or into tiny bite-size pieces to make petits fours. Store any leftovers in the refrigerator, wrapped in foil, for up to 3 days.

For gingered fruit bars, make the chocolate mix as above and stir in crushed graham crackers instead of the rich tea biscuits. Omit the nuts and use ⅓ cup ready-to-eat dried apricots, coarsely chopped, and 2 tablespoons chopped candied ginger, keeping 2–3 tablespoons back for the topping. **Calories per serving 351**

hot caribbean fruit salad

Calories per serving **408**
Serves **4**
Preparation time **15 minutes**
Cooking time **6–7 minutes**

3½ tablespoons **unsalted butter**
¼ cup firmly packed **light brown sugar**
1 **large papaya**, halved, seeded, peeled, and sliced
1 **large mango**, pitted, peeled, and sliced
½ **pineapple**, cored, peeled, and cut into chunks
1⅔ cups **full-fat coconut milk**
grated zest and juice of 1 **lime**

Heat the butter in a large skillet, add the sugar, and heat gently until just dissolved. Add all the fruit and cook for 2 minutes, then pour in the coconut milk, half the lime zest and all the juice.

Heat gently for 4–5 minutes, then serve warm in shallow bowls, sprinkled with the remaining lime zest.

For flamed Caribbean fruit salad, omit the coconut milk and add 3 tablespoons dark or white rum. When the rum is bubbling, flame with a long match and stand well back. When the flames have subsided, add the lime zest and juice and serve. **Calories per serving 252**

pistachio & yogurt semifreddo

Calories per serving **416**

Serves **6**

Preparation time **40 minutes**,
  plus cooling and freezing

Cooking time **10–15 minutes**

4 **eggs**, separated

generous ¾ cup **superfine
  sugar**

grated zest of 1 **lemon**

1½ teaspoons **rose water**
  (optional)

¾ cup **Greek yogurt**

½ **fresh pineapple**, sliced,
  halved, and cored

Pistachio brittle

¾ cup **sugar**

6 tablespoons **water**

1 cup **pistachio nuts**, roughly
  chopped

Make the brittle. Heat the sugar and measured water in a skillet until it dissolves, stirring gently from time to time. Add the nuts, then increase the heat and boil the syrup for 5 minutes, without stirring, until pale golden. Quickly tip the mixture onto a greased baking sheet and let cool. Break the brittle in half, then crush half in a plastic bag with a rolling pin.

Whisk the egg whites until very stiff, then gradually whisk in half the sugar until thick and glossy. Whisk the egg yolks in a second bowl with the remaining sugar until very thick and pale and the mixture leaves a trail. Fold in the lemon zest and rose water, if using, then the yogurt and crushed brittle, then the egg whites. Pour into a plastic box and freeze for 4–5 hours until semi-frozen and firm enough to scoop.

Cook the pineapple slices on a hot barbecue or preheated ridged grill pan for 6–8 minutes, turning once or twice until browned. Divide among the serving plates, top with spoonfuls of semifreddo, and decorate with broken pieces of the remaining brittle.

For rocky road ice cream, make the brittle with almonds, hazelnuts, and pecan nuts instead of pistachios. Whisk the egg whites, then the eggs and sugar, as for the semifreddo, then fold ½ cup store-bought custard and ⅔ cup whipped heavy cream into the yolks with the crushed brittle. Fold in the egg whites as above, then freeze. Serve scooped into glasses. **Calories per serving 410**

summer berry sponge

Calories per serving **422**

Serves **6**

Preparation time **30 minutes**, plus cooling

Cooking time **10–12 minutes**

4 **eggs**

½ cup **superfine sugar**

¾ cup **all-purpose flour**

finely grated zest and 2 tablespoons juice of 1 **lemon**

⅔ cup **heavy cream**

⅔ cup **fromage frais** or **plain yogurt**

3 tablespoons **lemon curd**

3 cups small **strawberries**, halved

1½ cups **blueberries**

4 tablespoons **red currant jelly**

1 tablespoon **water** (or **lemon juice**)

Whisk the eggs and superfine sugar in a large bowl until very thick and the mixture leaves a trail when lifted. Sift the flour over the surface of the eggs, then fold in very gently. Add the lemon zest and juice and fold in until just mixed. Pour the batter into a greased, floured 10 inch sponge flan pan, tilting the pan to ease into an even layer.

Bake in a preheated oven, at 350°F, for 10–12 minutes, until the top is golden and the center springs back when lightly pressed. Cool in the pan for 5–10 minutes, then carefully turn it out onto a wire rack to cool.

Whip the cream until it forms soft swirls, then fold in the fromage frais and lemon curd. Transfer the sponge flan to a serving plate, spoon the cream into the center, spread into an even layer, then top with the strawberries and blueberries. Warm the red currant jelly in a small saucepan with the measured water (or lemon juice), then brush over the fruit.

For strawberry sponge flan with Pimm's, make the sponge flan as above, then fill with 1¼ cups whipped cream flavored with the grated zest of ½ orange. Top with 3 cups sliced strawberries and 1¼ cups raspberries that have been soaked in 3 tablespoons undiluted Pimm's and 2 tablespoons sugar for 30 minutes. **Calories per serving 491**

toffee peaches

Calories per serving **424**
Serves **4**
Preparation time **10 minutes**
Cooking time **15 minutes**

4 **peaches**, halved and pitted
½ cup **ground almonds**

Sauce
½ cup firmly packed **light
   brown sugar**
5 tablespoons **maple syrup**
2 tablespoons **butter**
⅔ cup **light cream**

Cut 4 x 8 inch square pieces of foil and place 2 peach halves in each. Sprinkle over the ground almonds. Scrunch up the foil to form 4 parcels and place under a preheated medium broiler for 5–8 minutes, turning once or twice during cooking, until the peaches are soft.

Meanwhile, make the sauce. Place the sugar, maple syrup, and butter in a nonstick saucepan over moderately low heat until the sugar dissolves. Stir continuously until the sauce boils and thickens, which should take about 3 minutes. Add the cream and return to a boil, then immediately remove from the heat.

Drizzle the sauce over the peaches, and serve.

For toffee apples, place 4 halved apples in sheets of foil and divide 1 tablespoon butter between them in cubes, dotting over the top. Sprinkle with a little ground cinnamon and broil for 10–12 minutes, until the apples have softened, yet still retain their shape. Serve with the sauce as above. **Calories per serving 383**

pears with maple syrup cookies

Calories per serving **431**
Serves **4**
Preparation time **20 minutes**
Cooking time **50 minutes**

2 **vanilla beans**, split
3 tablespoons **honey**
1½ cups **sweet white wine**
⅔ cup **superfine sugar**
¾ cup **water**
4 **hard pears**, such as
  Packham or Comice, peeled,
  cored, and halved

Maple syrup cookies
2 tablespoons **reduced-fat
  sunflower spread**
2 tablespoons **maple syrup**
1 tablespoon **superfine sugar**
⅓ cup **all-purpose flour**
1 **egg white**

Combine the vanilla beans, honey, wine, sugar, and water in a saucepan large enough to hold all the pears. Heat until the sugar dissolves and then add the pears. Simmer for 30 minutes or until the pears are very tender. Remove the pears from the pan with a slotted spoon and set aside.

Simmer the syrup for about 15 minutes, until it has reduced. Set aside with the pears until ready to serve.

Make the cookies. Beat together the sunflower spread, maple syrup, and sugar, then stir in the flour. Beat the egg white until softly peaking, then fold it into the mix.

Drop teaspoonfuls of the mixture onto a lightly greased baking sheet, spacing the cookies well apart. Bake in a preheated oven, at 400°F, for about 8 minutes, until golden. Remove and transfer to a rack to cool.

Decorate the pears with a sliver of vanilla bean and serve with a little syrup drizzled over them and a cookie on the side.

For vanilla & rose water peaches, replace the pears with the same quantity of peaches and poach in the syrup as above for about 20 minutes or until tender. Halved peaches will take less time. Remove the peaches and continue to simmer the syrup for about 15 minutes, until it has reduced. Add 1–2 tablespoons rose water, to taste, for a more fragrant syrup. Finish as above. **Calories per serving 420**

toffee & banana pancakes

Calories per serving **438**

Serves **6**

Preparation time **15 minutes**,
   plus resting

Cooking time **30 minutes**

¾ cup **all-purpose flour**

pinch **salt**

1 **egg**

1 **egg yolk**

1¼ cups **milk**

2–3 tablespoons **sunflower oil**

2 **bananas**, sliced

Toffee sauce

3½ tablespoons **unsalted butter**

¼ cup firmly packed **light brown sugar**

2 tablespoons **light corn syrup**

⅔ cup **heavy cream**

Sift the flour into a bowl, add the salt, egg, and egg yolk, then gradually whisk in the milk to make a smooth batter. Set aside for 30 minutes.

Put the butter, sugar, and syrup for the toffee sauce in a small saucepan and heat gently, stirring occasionally, until the butter has melted and the sugar dissolved. Bring to a boil and cook for 3–4 minutes, until just beginning to darken around the edges.

Take the pan off the heat, then gradually pour in the cream. Tilt the pan to mix and as the bubbles subside stir with a wooden spoon. Set aside.

Pour the oil for cooking the pancakes into a 7 inch skillet, heat and then pour off the excess into a small bowl. Pour a little pancake batter over the bottom of the pan, tilt the pan to coat the bottom evenly with batter, then cook for 2 minutes, until the underside is golden. Loosen with a spatula, turn over and cook the second side in the same way. When cooked, slide onto a plate and keep hot. Cook the remaining batter, oiling the pan as needed.

Fold the pancakes and arrange on serving plates. Top with banana slices and drizzle with the toffee sauce.

For citrus pancakes, make the pancakes as above, then drizzle them with the freshly squeezed juice of 1 lemon and 1 orange. Sprinkle with ¼ cup sugar before serving. **Calories per serving 200**

cherries with cinnamon crumble

Calories per serving **440**
Serves **4–6**
Preparation time **15 minutes**,
  plus cooling
Cooking time **20 minutes**

3 lb **cherries**, pitted
1 ¼ cups **sugar**
1 ⅔ cups **water**
1 **vanilla bean**
2 **cloves**
strips of **orange peel**,
  to decorate

Crumble
2 oz **fruit loaf**
1 tablespoon **unsalted butter**
⅛ teaspoon **ground
  cinnamon**
1 tablespoon **sugar**

Cinnamon cream
1 tablespoon **confectioners'
  sugar**
⅔ cup **whipping cream**
¼ teaspoon **ground
  cinnamon**

Put the cherries in a large bowl. Place the sugar in a heavy saucepan and add the measured water, vanilla bean, cloves, and orange peel. Bring to a boil, stirring occasionally, then pour the syrup over the cherries. Let cool.

Make the crumble. Cut the fruit loaf into ½ inch dice. Melt the butter and drizzle it over the fruit loaf. Mix together the cinnamon and sugar and sprinkle over the fruit loaf. Mix well, transfer to a baking sheet, and cook in a preheated oven, at 375°F, for 4–5 minutes, until golden and crunchy. Remove the crumble from the oven and let cool.

Meanwhile, make the cinnamon cream. Sift the confectioners' sugar over the cream, add the cinnamon, and whip until firm peaks form.

Serve the cherries with a small amount of syrup, a spoonful of the cinnamon cream, and a sprinkling of the fruit loaf crumble. Decorate with strips of orange peel.

pink grapefruit cream

Calories per serving **463** (not
    including brandy snaps)
Serves **4**
Preparation time **15 minutes**

2 **pink grapefruits**
5 tablespoons firmly packed
    dark brown sugar, plus
    extra for sprinkling
1 cup **heavy cream**
²/₃ cup **Greek yogurt**
3 tablespoons **concentrated
    elderflower cordial**
½ teaspoon **ground ginger**
½ teaspoon **ground
    cinnamon**
brandy snaps, to serve
    (optional)

Grate the zest of 1 grapefruit finely, making sure you
don't take any of the bitter white pith. Cut the skin
and the white membrane off both grapefruits, and cut
between the membranes to remove the segments.
Place in a large dish, sprinkle with 2 tablespoons of
the sugar and set aside.

Whip the cream in a large bowl until thick but not stiff.
Fold in the yogurt, elderflower cordial, spices, grapefruit
zest, and remaining sugar until smooth.

Spoon the mixture into attractive glasses, arranging the
grapefruit segments between layers of grapefruit cream.
Sprinkle the top with a little extra sugar, add the brandy
snaps, if desired, and serve immediately.

For spiced orange cream, finely grate the zest of
2 large oranges, then cut away the pith and membrane
to release the orange segments. Sprinkle with
2 tablespoons of the sugar and set aside. Whip the
cream, then flavor as above, adding the orange zest in
place of the grapefruit zest. **Calories per serving 472**

pear, apple & cinnamon crumble

Calories per serving **465**
Serves **6**
Preparation time **10 minutes**
Cooking time **30–35 minutes**

1½ lb **pears**, peeled, cored,
  and sliced
1 lb **cooking apples**, peeled,
  cored, and sliced
2 tablespoons firmly packed
  light brown sugar
1 teaspoon **ground cinnamon**
¼ cup **apple juice**

Topping
1¼ cups **rice flour**
7 tablespoons **butter**, cubed
½ cup firmly packed **light
  brown sugar**
¼ cup **sliced almonds**
3 tablespoons **blanched
  hazelnuts**, roughly chopped

Put the pears and apples in a large saucepan with the sugar, cinnamon, and apple juice. Cover and cook gently, stirring occasionally, for about 10 minutes or until the fruit is just tender. Transfer to an ovenproof dish.

Make the topping. Place the flour and butter in a food processor and process until the mixture resembles fine bread crumbs. Alternatively, place the flour in a large bowl, add the butter and blend in with the fingertips until the mixture resembles fine bread crumbs. Stir in the sugar and nuts, then sprinkle over the fruit and press down gently.

Place in a preheated oven, at 400°F, for 20–25 minutes, until golden and bubbling.

For rhubarb & ginger crumble, cut 2 lb rhubarb into chunks and put in an ovenproof dish with 2 tablespoons water and 6 tablespoons sugar. Place in a preheated oven, at 400°F, for 15 minutes, then stir in 1 teaspoon ground ginger. Make the topping as above, adding 3½ oz finely chopped marzipan. Sprinkle over the rhubarb and bake in the oven as above. **Calories per serving 497**

berry meringue mess

Calories per serving **467**
Serves **6**
Preparation time **10 minutes**
Cooking time **1 hour**

4 **egg whites**
1 cup **superfine sugar**
1 teaspoon **white wine vinegar**
1¼ cups **heavy cream**
2¼ cups **raspberries**, plus extra, left whole, to decorate
1½ cups **strawberries**, hulled and quartered, plus extra, left whole and unhulled, to decorate
2 tablespoons **confectioners' sugar**
2 tablespoons **cream liqueur**

Line 2 large baking sheets with nonstick parchment paper.

Whisk the egg whites in a large clean bowl until they form stiff peaks. Add the sugar a spoonful at a time and continue to whisk until thick and glossy. Fold in the vinegar with a large metal spoon.

Spoon or pipe 12 meringues onto the prepared baking sheets. Place in a preheated oven, at 300°F, for 1 hour, then switch off the oven and leave the meringues inside to cool completely. When cool, roughly crush the meringues.

Whip the cream in a large bowl until it forms soft peaks. Roughly crush together the raspberries and strawberries and stir into the cream. Fold in the crushed meringues, confectioners' sugar, and cream liqueur. Spoon into 6 tall glasses, decorate with extra whole berries, and serve immediately.

For mango & passion fruit mess, make the meringues as above and roughly crush. Whip the cream with 2 tablespoons confectioners' sugar in a large bowl until it forms soft peaks. Peel and pit 1 large mango and puree half the flesh in a food processor or blender. Chop the remaining mango flesh and stir all the mango into the cream mixture with the scooped flesh of 2 passion fruit. Fold in the crushed meringues and serve immediately. **Calories per serving 475**

baked apples & oat crumble

Calories per serving **488**
(not including ice cream or
reduced-fat sour cream)
Serves **4**
Preparation time **15 minutes**
Cooking time **20–25 minutes**

4 **dessert apples**, halved and
cored
½ cup **raisins**
¼ cup **light corn syrup**
6 tablespoons **apple juice**
or **water**
⅓ cup **all-purpose flour**
½ cup **rolled oats**
¼ cup firmly packed **light
brown sugar**
3½ tablespoons **unsalted
butter**, at room temperature,
diced
2 tablespoons **sunflower
seeds**
2 tablespoons **sesame seeds**
vanilla ice cream or
reduced-fat sour cream, to
serve (optional)

Arrange the apples, cut side up, in a shallow ovenproof
dish. Divide the raisins among the apples, pressing them
into the core cavity. Drizzle with 2 tablespoons of the
light corn syrup and add the apple juice or water to the
bottom of the dish.

Put the flour, oats, sugar, and butter into a small bowl
and blend the butter with fingertips until the mixture
resembles fine bread crumbs. Stir in the seeds. Spoon
the crumble over the top of the apples and mound up.
Drizzle with the remaining syrup.

Cook in a preheated oven, at 350°F, for 20–25 minutes,
until the crumble is golden and the apples are soft.
Serve warm with scoops of vanilla ice cream or
reduced-fat sour cream, if desired.

For plum & muesli crumble, halve 10 plums and
place them, cut side up, in an ovenproof dish. Drizzle
with 2 tablespoons honey and add 6 tablespoons red
grape juice or water to the bottom of the dish. Make
the crumble, using 1 cup of muesli instead of the oats
and seeds. Bake and serve as above. **Calories per
serving 393**

flourless chocolate cake

Calories per serving **488**
Cuts into **12**
Preparation time **25 minutes**
Cooking time **1 hour**

scant 1 cup **blanched
  almonds**, roughly chopped
1 cup **Brazil nuts**, roughly
  chopped
8 oz **semisweet chocolate**,
  chopped into ¼ inch pieces
2 sticks **slightly salted butter**,
  softened
4 **eggs**, separated
generous 1 cup **unrefined
  superfine sugar**
sifted **unsweetened cocoa
  powder**, for dusting

Put the almonds, Brazil nuts, and chocolate in a food processor and process until the consistency of ground almonds. Beat together the butter, egg yolks, and ¾ cup of the sugar in a bowl until pale and creamy. Stir in the chocolate mixture.

Whisk the egg whites in a large clean bowl with a handheld electric mixer until peaking. Gradually whisk in the remaining sugar, a spoonful at a time. Stir a quarter of the mixture into the creamed mixture using a large metal spoon. Add the remaining egg whites and stir gently to mix.

Spoon the mixture into a greased and lined 9 inch removable-bottomed or springform cake pan and level the surface. Bake in a preheated oven, at 325°F, for about 1 hour or until just firm to the touch and a toothpick inserted into the center comes out clean.

Let cool in the pan (the center of the cake will sink slightly), then remove the ring and base and dust with sifted cocoa powder. Serve with fresh raspberry compote, if desired (see below).

For fresh raspberry compote, to serve as an accompaniment, put ½ cup fresh raspberries, 3 tablespoons sugar, 1 teaspoon vanilla extract, and 1 tablespoon water in a small saucepan. Cook for about 5 minutes, until the raspberries are soft and mushy. Strain through a sieve into a bowl and stir in another 2 cups raspberries. Mix gently until coated in the sauce. Chill until ready to serve. **Calories per serving 21**

autumn fruit oaty crumble

Calories per serving **495**
Serves **4**
Preparation time **15 minutes**
Cooking time **40–45 minutes**

1 **dessert apple**, peeled,
   cored, and sliced
1 oz ready-to-eat **dried
   apples**, chopped (optional)
13 oz can **pear halves** in
   juice, drained and roughly
   chopped, with ¼ cup juice
   reserved
7 oz **ripe plums**, halved,
   pitted, and quartered
2 tablespoons **raisins** or
   golden raisins
¼ cup **fat-free Greek yogurt**,
   to serve (optional)

Topping
generous ½ cup **whole-wheat
   flour**
½ cup **rolled oats**
¼ cup **bran**
pinch of **salt**
½ cup **pecan nuts**, chopped
2 tablespoons firmly packed
   dark brown sugar
¾ teaspoon **mixed spice**
5 tablespoons **butter**, melted

Put all the prepared fruit and raisins into a shallow, rectangular ovenproof dish, approximately 11 x 8 inches. Drizzle over the reserved pear juice.

Mix together the dry topping ingredients in a large bowl. Pour over the melted butter and combine until the mixture resembles large bread crumbs. Sprinkle over the fruit and press down firmly.

Place in a preheated oven, at 350°F, for 40–45 minutes or until golden and crisp. Serve with 1 tablespoon fat-free Greek yogurt per person, if desired.

For forest fruit & clementine crumble, replace the fresh and dried fruits with 1 lb frozen forest fruits, thawed and drained of excess liquid. Slice 2 clementines into segments, discarding the pith, and mix with the forest fruits. Spread the fruit over the bottom of the ovenproof dish, cover with the crumble topping, and bake as above. Serve with 1 tablespoon fat-free Greek yogurt per person, if desired. Calories per serving 438

index

acknowledgments

Commissioning editor: Eleanor Maxfield
Senior editor: Ellie Smith
Editor: Pollyanna Poulter
Designer: Jeremy Tilston
Production controller: Allison Gonsalves
Americanizer: Nicole Foster

Photography: Octopus Publishing Group Limited 18–19; Stephen Conroy 6–7, 115, 139, 157, 177, 179, 181, 187; Will Heap 4–5, 8, 10, 11 left, 12 left, 12 right, 13, 21, 23, 27, 31, 39, 49, 55, 57, 63, 67, 83, 99, 119, 129, 131, 133, 145, 161, 195, 205, 207, 211, 213, 215, 221, 231; David Munns 123, 151, 169; Emma Neish 109; Lis Parsons 11 right, 15, 25, 35, 51, 61, 73, 75, 77, 81, 85, 87, 91, 93, 97, 117, 125, 141, 149, 185, 193, 197, 199, 203, 209, 217, 219, 223, 225; Gareth Sambidge 47, 147, 191; William Shaw 1, 2–3, 9, 29, 33, 37, 41, 43, 45, 53, 59, 65, 69, 78–79, 95, 101, 103, 105, 107, 111, 113, 121, 127, 135, 137, 153, 155, 162–163, 165, 167, 171, 173, 175, 189, 200–201, 227, 229, 233, 235; Ian Wallace 71, 89, 143, 159, 183.